Praise for The Ugly

"I was so glad I read *The Ugly Couch* and entered Tonyland for a while. I appreciate Tony's raw honesty as he shares his life and lessons learned in his journey toward true identity. I was encouraged about the Father's heart for me, His grace toward me, and have given thought to which rooms the ugly couches are residing in my own life. You too will be challenged by his truth, uplifted by his hilarious stories, and you will identify with his wounds and know that you're not alone as you read, *The Ugly Couch*."

- Darrell Evans
Beloved songwriter and lead worshipper of Jesus.
A pioneer in modern worship music.

Mikel,
Your support means more to me than you realize. I hope this book is an encouragement to you!

Tony Mathe

THE UGLY COUCH
Learning When To Throw Things Away

Tony Ziolko

The Ugly Couch Copyright © 2014 by Tony Ziolko
Printed in the United States of America

ISBN 978-0-9863407-0-3
eISBN 978-0-9863407-1-0
Library of Congress Control Number: 2015900700

Book cover design by Chris Pahls
www.chrispahls.squarespace.com

Manuscript editing by James Watkins
wordpress.jameswatkins.com/news/editing/

This book is a work of nonfiction. Some names, businesses, organizations, places, and events have been concealed for their protection. Any resemblance to actual persons, living or dead, events, or locales is entirely coincidental. Any real life story is portrayed from the perspective of the author. No intentional misperceptions of situations and people intended.

The font "Blanch" was used as the main typeface for the book cover and for all chapter titles. The font "Blanch" was downloaded from the website www.losttype.com and was designed and created by Atipus. They can be found at www.atipus.com

This book is dedicated to my beautiful children,
Aubrie and Drake.
I am a better man because of you both.

For more ramblings, feel free to visit

www.theuglycouch.com

And if you don't . . . fine . . . whatever. I don't care.
I don't like you anyway.

CONTENTS

ACKNOWLEDGMENTS

My wife, Ashley

There's always a certain level of love you expect from your spouse because, well, you have to support them. Not from you. You truly believe in me and support my crazy visions. You inspire me to be successful in everything I do. You are my sanity. You are my Super Glue. I fall in love with you more and more everyday. I think you are hot and super sexy! Thank you for being the way the Holy Spirit talks to me!

My mother

My foundation, my shield. Words cannot describe your value in my life. You are the reason I love God. You are the reason I am so strong. I have your passion and creativity, and I thank you for that. Your strength amazes me, and I love my children better than I every imagined possible because of the way you loved me.

My step-dad, Pat

What a blessing you are to me and our family. I see God's love in you as I watch you love me, mom, and our family. You are a special man, and I am blessed to call you dad. I can't wait to enjoy the rest of our lives together.

My in-laws

I don't know what else to say, other than to thank you for being the blessing you both have been in my life. I feel so lucky to have in-laws so supportive and easy to have a relationship with. You truly are my family.

My family

There are too many of you to list, but I love you all. You all have influenced and inspired my life. I am honored to have you all in my life.

My therapist

Thank you for helping me process all my craziness. Life can seem unfair sometimes, but you helped me see that what seems unfair, can actually be a blessing if I choose to allow God make it such. You changed my life more than you probably realize. Our sessions weren't anything out of the ordinary for you, but to me, they were life-changing.

Chris Pahls

Of course, thank you for the book cover design and everything else you helped with on this book. But that's not why I'm acknowledging you. I cherish your friendship. The way you serve with me in ministry, so selflessly and with such talent; never asking for anything in return. You are way more talented than me, and I love it. You are the most valuable tool God has given me in my current ministry, and I'm stoked to be on staff with you. Everything from your music, designing, filming to your pastoral heart. The way you keep me "in check" when I go to say or do something stupid and the way you challenge the standard way of thinking is so refreshing. Oh, and your beard is superb.

Dave Henry

I say some stupid things sometimes. I have some crazy ideas, and I'm really young and reckless at times. But you don't see that. You see my heart. You are one of the most gentle, humble, and wisest men I know. I am honored to serve under you, and I am blessed you saw a pastor in such a young guy and not a punk kid who thinks he knows everything.

Starbucks

Thank you for your delicious coffee and for giving me a change of scenery to write and work when I needed to get out of the house and office or when I wanted people to see me writing so I could feel more important than I actually am. I thank you for your environment. An environment where I can take my daughter on Princess Dates to eat Cake Pops. You're more than a coffee shop; you provide a place where people can do life together and just simply experience life.

SPECIAL HONORS

This book could not have been made possible if it weren't for those people who believed in me. I funded my project through Kickstarter, and this is a list of those people who contributed financially in me and my project. You all gave sacrificially to my work, and I could not be more grateful. You all are incredible! Thank you for being my "investors." May God pour an extra blessing onto your lives for your selfless and sacrificial giving.

My backers:
Jonathan and Lauren Atkins
Tobin and Amber Sawyers
Ron and Deb Hustus
Pat and Brenda Keller
Todd and Wendi Rehn
Bob and Vickey Simmons
Dan and Stacy Sell
Chris and Alina Kolp
Bob and Janet Pahls
Sal and Carol Schamante
Tyson and Katie Swank
Doug and Esther Kempton
Brandon and Krystal Church
Rob Polifka
Jen Derickson
Chris and Amanda Pahls

Isaac and Shannon Taylor
Jesse Yarochowicz
Tacoma and Jennifer Zach
Dave and Lena Ogershok
Gabe and Dawn Foster
Melissa Buhrle
Jacob Penvose
Whitney Bailey
Holli Polito
Gregg and Yvonne Leake
John and Sharon Miller
Brad and Robin Burr
Aaron Hoover
Caden Baughman
Cindy Dunning
Debra Edwards
Mark Cowin
Joel Parker
Adam and Lacy Paredes
Leroy and Nancy Keller
Chris and Cindy Gearheart
Michelle Keller
Fred and Renee Corn
Mike Perkins
Nathan Rishel
DJ McAninch
Mark and Deanna Erikson
DeAnn Cornwell
Tucker Dowling

Frank and Linda Shipkowski
Kenny Elder
Corey and Brianne Errett
TJ and Gina Turner
Matthew and Rindi Guldner
Brad and Cassandra Shields
Kali McMahon
Bryson and Marlee Isom
Brandon and Ashley Reiter
Dave and Michelle Henry

INTRODUCTION

I know what you're thinking. *Who are you and why should I care what you say?* I know that's what you're thinking, because I read a book on how to write a book that told me that's what people think when reading a book. And if that book is anything like Wikipedia; it must be true.

Here are a few things to consider while reading:
I didn't spend eighty grand to get my doctorate, extensively study these subjects, or sit on the floor of my living room in a monk robe, but I have faith that God will use this material for its true intention.

This book is not a theological decree. I am not standing on these words as absolute truth, and you shouldn't accept them as that. I'm a human who loves Jesus and wants to love people *like* Jesus. I'm a screw up like the rest of us, and these are just a few things I've learned or contemplated as my faith has matured.

Trust me, if you hold this book up to a theological scholar, you will be sadly disappointed. Take the things I say in this book and decide on your own to agree or disagree with me.

This book is transparent. It is raw and it is real. So there may be a few things I say that may cause you to get a little irritated at me. Don't send the torches and pitch fork riots to my house. I always have a point, so hear me out.

Finally, I'm not an official spokesperson for Starbucks, nor are they paying me to advertise for them. After completing this book, I realized I talked a lot about Starbucks. Here's the deal: *I just love Starbucks.*

Who am I?

I am a young father, husband, and pastor. I care way too much about how my hair looks, and I suffer from Obsessive Compulsive Disorder (OCD). If you cut me open, I would bleed coffee and I cuss probably more than heaven allows a pastor to cuss; so there's that. I don't want to split hairs, but in my defense, I don't say the "really bad" ones; I just think them like everyone else. I love heavy metal music, and I'm not talking about *Twisted Sister* or *Slipknot* kind of *"metal."* I'm talking the real stuff. The heavy metal music that is so heavy, your bones feel the gravitational pull from the low, heavy tones of the guitars and screams of the vocalists. Bands like *Parkway Drive, For Today* and *August Burns Red*

I have a beautiful wife who loves and supports my crazy, big visions, and I have a daughter that fulfills my mother's prophesy of, "Oh just wait until you have your own kids, then you'll understand." Also, my son is rad.

I graduated with a bachelors degree which may surprise you, since I listen to heavy metal. I studied Political Science before I realized that I didn't want to work eighty hours a week and have two separate homes. After interning with an elected official, I realized the political sphere was not for me. In the process, I also attempted a ministry degree. However, I didn't feel good about paying thirty grand per year to have my professors tell me to read Rob Bell and Francis Chan books, then debate them when I could do that with friends. By the way, Francis Chan wins . . . every time. But I did finally settle on a Public Management degree. It was a happy medium between politics and ministry which we all know, you can't have ministry without some politics!

I am a pastor and currently get the privilege to help pastor a church in Kansas. I've ministered in churches in Phoenix before pastoring in Kansas and, before becoming a pastor, I've served in leadership roles as a volunteer in churches in Pennsylvania and Indiana. At the moment, I'm an associate pastor with my primary responsibility being the worship arts. I've been leading worship, at the moment I write this, for ten years. I will say that the first three years probably shouldn't count because I was in high school and terrible at it.

Why should you care what I say?

You really shouldn't care what I say, but I am as regular of a person as there can be. So I feel like that should count for something. My life experiences are real, raw, and probably connect with more people than I realize.

As I was processing through the material of this book, one theme kept coming to me. So I decided it would be a chapter in the book—only to wake up one day just absolutely hating the working title I had for the book and website. I thought it was lame and cheesy, and I don't want to be lame and cheesy. I want to be a hipster who wears oversized glasses and undersized jeans. But I can't, because I'm chubby and chubby guys in skinny jeans don't benefit anyone.

I scratched off the working title on my book notes and continued writing without a title. As I proceeded with the writing of this particular chapter, on the theme I was thinking about, I decided to title the chapter "The Ugly Couch." Then about half-way through the chapter, I realized that the overarching theme of the chapter seemed to be indicative of my entire life—and most of the other chapters I had been already been working on. I got excited and decided the new name of the book would be *The Ugly Couch: Learning When to Throw Stuff Away.*

So what does it mean? Well, it all started in my grandma's living room. My grandma had two living rooms. One living room where the TV and the recliners were and the other living room was big, full of couches, an organ, a piano, a gun safe, and pictures of the family all around the room. There were so many couches and chairs in her living room, and none of them matched. They were all really ugly and beyond outdated.

It always baffled me as to why she had so many unmatched couches. But behind each couch and chair was a story, and they had owned each one of those couches for a long time. The couches were well-worn and just a part of my grandparents identity.

We all know of them, whether it is at a grandparents house or at another place. We walk in, wherever it is at, and see it—

that hideous piece of furniture. Maybe it's not a couch specifically. Maybe it's a dresser, or maybe it's the carpet. Maybe it's the armoire or the wallpaper. Either way, we can all agree that no matter what the item is, it needs to go. And preferably go to the landfill on the other side of the country. In fact, we wouldn't even want to take up space at the landfill with these items. We should probably just set fire to them and burn them straight to ash.

The problem with these "ugly couches" or pieces of furniture are that the owners usually love them. I know from my experiences, they have usually had them for many, many years and, to them, they're beautiful. There is usually a grand story behind each one that they just love to laugh about, meanwhile, you are laughing at them. They claim that it's a part of who they are and proudly display the item, but to everyone else it is blindingly hideous.

We all have these hideous things in our lives. Maybe they are pride, arrogance, ignorance, selfishness, or negativity. Maybe they are the addictions we are unaware of, the way we talk to people, the language we use, our lack of social awareness, or how we brag that we haven't read a book since high school. But chances are, if the last one is you, you're probably not even reading this book, so I could potentially say whatever I want about you right now and you would never know. "Hey person who hasn't read a book since high school, you smell like old mayonnaise."

But whatever these things are, we all have them. We claim they are just a part of us, but really we're just to blinded to how ugly they really are. We get comfortable with these things and easily identify them as "just how God made us." Maybe we are aware of how ugly our "couches" are, but that couch is comfortable to us, and we are afraid to take the time to break in a new one. Truth be told, some of our couches are just ugly; and sometimes, we need to learn when to throw the ugly couches away.

These stories are a collection of my ugly couches. These are all idiotic characteristics, choices, and mindsets that have hindered me as a person, and my hope is that you can use my ugly couches as a caution sign to avoid. Or maybe you will identify with these things and my experiences will encourage you to throw your ugly couches away, too.

THE FLIP-FLOP

I once thought I was gay. It was a fleeting thought, but it existed nonetheless. While doctors think it's because of my tragic past, others tend to think that it has something to do with my TV show obsession, *Gossip Girl* and *Pretty Little Liars.* I have always been drawn to more feminine things. And just in full disclosure, I used to spend $120 for a haircut and highlights. And yes, I used a hair straightener. It was really worth it, until I got married and had to pay rent. Growing up, I had an older sister, and a younger sister, and no brothers. I always played Barbies with them, and they would use me as their mannequin to sample clothes and make-up. Of course, I didn't know any better. However, I do believe with the entirety of my soul that an evil plan to make fun of me was behind their innocent faces.

But something was present in my life—and something was lacking—and I think I figured it out. I lacked the masculine gene. If you don't believe me, use this book as a reference.

"Real men" don't write books, they watch UFC fights and spit. I think spitting is gross, and it makes me thirsty. And UFC fights . . . well, I don't like getting shots at the doctors, so why would I want to watch someone get a knee to the face or get their shoulder dislocated? But honestly; if you want to see the height of my masculinity, just show me a spider.

Mike the bully

I grew up in a small rural town in the rolling hills of Pennsylvania that consisted of eight thousand people. There was an unspoken event in my high school that quickly got shut down after a series of predictable events—kind of like a Vin Diesel film. The event was a "freshman beat down day." I don't exactly remember what they called it, but a group of upperclassman decided it would be a great idea to have a day where they would scare and pummel freshman. I remember being a freshman and walking the white-washed hallways terrified. I had a sense of security because my sister was an upperclassman, and I knew her friends would look out for me, but there was still that doubt that in my time alone, I would turn the corner to my death.

Now entering the story is Mike. He was an upperclassman and was a giant bully. I remember during a freshman beat down day, Mike walked up to a kid, right in front of a teacher, and punched the kid square in the face. I didn't say he was smart, but he was a kid to fear. He was a great athlete all around and could kick anyone's "behind" to China. I heard tales of his conquests, and I went into my "freshman beat down day" nothing short of trembling. And since I lacked the masculine gene, I made for the perfect target. I remember standing at my locker with my friend when Mike walked right up to me and in a surprisingly non-threatening way said to me, "Are you [my dad's name] kid?"

"Yes," I sheepishly replied.

"Well, you're cool with me then." Then he walked away. He just walked away! I was shocked and excited at the same time. Then it dawned on me why he walked away. It was because of my dad. And that was just one moment where my dad, my super hero, came through for me and saved the day.

Superhero Dad

He was a big guy, my dad. Huge to be honest. I was quite proud to call him my dad. In elementary school, most competitions on the playgrounds between the kids turned into shouting matches about which dad could beat up the others dad. My friends at school knew that getting into that battle with me was an inevitable losing situation. The last number that I can remember that my dad bench pressed was three hundred and fifty pounds before he had to have shoulder surgery. That's a lot of weight for a short, stalky, Italian guy who didn't even weigh two hundred pounds.

One of the fondest memories of my dad was watching him at the gym. I remember going to the gym with him as a kid. And not those lame gyms with all the pulley system machines and all the ellipticals. This was a ghetto gym that still had the old rusty chains and played Def Leppard tunes. This wasn't a cardio gym. This was a gym for the tough. This was a *man's* gym. In fact the gym was so tough that its name was seriously called The Bod Shop. Sounds like a place the dudes from *Jersey Shore* would go after tanning.

I would sit behind the sign-in desk with the black and white TV, and I would watch him intently, with his huge lifting belt and even bigger biceps. There was also a room upstairs that was just a big square room with a punching bag in the middle. I would run up the stairs when Eye of the Tiger would come on the radio, and I would hit the bag profusely as if I were beating up Apollo Creed.

There were even times when dad would help me lift. I would grab the five-pound dumbbells (maybe they were two pounders, but I think five pounders sound better) and he would teach me to do bicep curls. Sometimes he would even ask me to spot him on the bench press. I would stand behind him and he would shout, "Up!" That was my signal to help him lift the weight off the rack. While he was lifting the weight, my job was to shout at him "Come on dad, you can do it! Don't be a wimp!" He told me to shout things like that because it was motivating. Then he would rack the weight, jump up, and make grunting noises. In between sets, we would both go over to the chalk bowl and chalk our hands. Of course, I didn't need to, but I did anyway.

As I got older, I realized he didn't really need me to spot him at all, and he was in fact, lifting weight he could have lifted with one hand. The grunts were merely an act to make me feel like I was actually contributing, but it was bliss. It was me and dad in the gym with the guys.

I admired my dad. I would watch him lift weights, watch him mow the yard, watch him eat, study how he made coffee, and of course, listened intently to his stories. He was more than my dad, he was my superhero and the superstar I admired. Some kids wanted to be firemen, policemen, or pro athletes. Not me. I wanted to be my dad. I wanted to bench press three hundred and fifty pounds, put chalk on my hands, make coffee with milk and four spoonfuls of sugar, listen to Air Supply, coach football, drive a truck, and get a tattoo that said "Italian Power." What he was, is what I wanted to be.

Flip-flops and Frostys

It was a chilly fall night, and I remember it vividly. I was sixteen years old, and the family sat down for dinner as we usually did when I broke the news. I started to explain to them I was auditioning for the all-school-musical *Beauty and the Beast*. I explained how I knew I could sing and that my friends kept encouraging me to audition.

To be completely honest, I was terrified to audition. I knew I could sing, but this was new territory for me. All I knew was sports at the time. I didn't really think I had a shot at getting cast as anything other than a chorus member. And let's be honest, if they cast you as a chorus member, that's their nice way of telling you you're terrible.

However, there was a dilemma. If I did the musical, it would require me to quit baseball. My whole life, in my pursuit to be like my dad, I had became a sports guy. I played sports and watched sports. That was it. Well, on the weekends, I would also watch Van Dam movies with my dad. The problem? I was not very good at sports. I played football and baseball ever since I was old enough to compete. Since I seemed to lack the masculine gene, this was the only avenue in which I could connect with my dad and try to make him proud. All I wanted the whole time was to make him proud, and I had already quit football at that point.

One of the main reasons I quit football in my sophomore year of high school was primarily because my role on the team. My title was literally "practice squad." After quitting football, I really felt like a failure. When I told my dad I quit football, he literally sulked, and as he sighed he said, "Well, at least we still have baseball." I remember that quote well for a reason. He used the word "we" whether it was intentional or not. My success was his success, and my failures were his failures. That was a heavy burden, and that was the dilemma. Now I had to break the news to him that we were quitting baseball.

As I concluded my sales pitch about why I thought audition-ing for the musical could be a great experience for me, I waited for his response. It was like when you text message someone something very important, and they don't reply right away. You start to panic and check your phone every ten seconds. He didn't really say anything at first; which was unusual. Then he finally spoke up, "When is it?"

"The first weekend in April, but auditions are in a month or two" I replied.

Then he asked the question I was hoping would get over-looked, "What about baseball?"

I paused and processed my response. Finally saying, "Well, it would be a January to April commitment. So it would be a gamble. I would have to quit baseball in order to audition and I'm not guaranteed a role."

"So, this is one of those singin' and twirlin' things?" he asked.

"Yes."

Then he said something that I will never forget for the rest of my life, and it has haunted me since that night. He said it with a joking tone, but it didn't matter if he was joking or not. It was evident that dad was disappointed in his son as he replied, "What, are you gay now?"

Everything I wanted to be, everything that I desired to do, everything I admired from watching him at the gym was an epic fail. I was confused. If those were the ingredients of being a man, I was a lost cause. I can't remember how long I sat there or what I said after that or if I said anything at all.

It was a warm Saturday on that following April of my junior year and nearly five, maybe six months had past since I told my dad that I was quitting baseball. I had in fact repressed that comment my dad made and auditioned for the musical anyway. I didn't think it went well, but it must have. I was cast as one of the main characters. I was Gaston in *Beauty and the Beast*. It was really exciting for me. I finally found something that I didn't have to sit on the bench for. I really dove into this new chapter of my life. I didn't know much about acting and dancing, but I did my best and I practiced a lot. I gave it my all, and I really feel like in that point of my life, I couldn't have given a better performance. Gaston was a big guy and I wasn't. So for this musical, I had to wear a muscle suit and an Elvis wig. I didn't care. I was so excited I was a main character that I would have worn high heels if I had to. *Okay, considering the topic of conversation right now, let's pretend I didn't say that.* Teachers actually told us that our cast was one of the best in ten years.

Saturday was our final night of performances, and I was feeling pretty good. I had just gotten my drivers license and I was killing it on the stage. Life was good. I decided to take my roadway freedoms out a little early that day. I decided I would stop at Wendy's on the way to the school and get myself one of those famous Frostys. On my way out of the house, my dad scolded me for wearing flip-flops while driving a stick-shift. I laughed it off. I arrived at the Wendy's drive-through and ordered a delicious Frosty. I retrieved my delicious treat and pulled out to leave. As I turned the corner, I was letting off of the clutch on the car and my flip-flop got caught on the floor mat. It came off. Well, since I was going like two miles per hour, I looked down and put it back on. Bad idea. I looked up and didn't see a road. I saw those miniature pine trees that line the building and saw the large glass window of the building. Some-how, within three seconds of looking down with a max speed of like two miles per hour, I managed to get my car to turn ninety degrees headed directly into the building.

It's interesting to me that I can't remember what I had for lunch last week, but I am able to remember this incident with such precise and vivid details. The details I am expressing, and the story I am telling are 100 percent true. You can't make this stuff up.

As I looked beyond the miniature pine trees, I saw my inevitable destination: the building and glass window. My eyes peered through the glass window and there was a lady. A very fat lady. This lady was in the process of putting—no, more like shoveling—a handful of french fries into her mouth when she glanced to the window and saw my beautiful face and awesome 1992 Honda Accord headed toward her. Without hesitation, the lady leaped out of her booth—with her fries. I proceeded to enter the building just underneath the giant window and through the fake brick wall, where I took out two booths. The entire front end of my car was literally inside Wendy's. Gives a new meaning to "drive-through," doesn't it? Now, either my car was ridiculously strong or that building was terribly weak, because my car literally went *through* a building and didn't get a scratch on it. I'm leaning toward the building being weak.

Well, as I sat in my car, *in* Wendy's, I contemplated backing out and driving away. I decided to leave the car inside the building, get out, and accept the consequences. Now, after thinking about it some more, I realized it would have been so awesome if I would have gotten out of my car and actually walked into the building through the hole I made. Too bad I always think of these things after the fact. But the story continues and gets better.

As I walked through the front door, with my Frosty and travel mug of tea, head hanging in shame, I heard laughter. The employees and customers were actually laughing. I looked up to see what was so funny, and it was me. As I stood there waiting for the manager, a family with a kid looked at me and the mom said, "Hey, aren't you Gaston from the musical?" and without giving me time to answer, she continued, "Susie, look! It's Gaston from *Beauty and the Beast!* Do you want his autograph?" The little girl said yes. I could see the headline on the front page of the local paper the next day: "Gaston helps Wendy's renovate drive-through. Signs autographs."

As I finished my autograph, the shift manager came out with a folder, laughing, and told me to have a seat. After asking if I wanted a fresh Frosty instead of my already melted one, he proceeded to ask me what happened. I explained myself, and he told me that he was going to have to call the police for insurance reasons, and that I would need to call one of my parents since I was still a minor. The first thing that came out of my mouth was, "My mom is going to kill me."

Mom was the disciplinarian. We kids knew dad was the cool one and mom was the scary one. I knew that my phone conversation would include an abundant amount of cuss words and that dreadful, high-pitched yell that made my stomach sick. I made the call and unfortunately, mom answered. I proceeded to explain my story again, and she didn't believe me. She laughed and told me to "shut up." She really thought I was joking, which made me realize how ridiculous my story really was. Once I finally insisted the story was true, and after she discovered that I was physically okay, her tone quickly changed, and she told me that I was in trouble in words that I cannot say if I wish to get this book published. When I told her one of them needed to come, she said she was sending my dad because she didn't have the patience for it. I was relieved. I wanted dad to come.

Some time later, the policeman and my dad showed up. My dad stood there and didn't say a word the whole time, while the policeman did his routine. That's when the next crazy part of the story happened. A huge black SUV came howling into the parking lot and this big bald man got out of the vehicle. Apparently he was the property owner or something, and he was not happy.

He started yelling and demanding that I get a drug test. It was absolutely ridiculous. I stood there as the bald man argued with the policeman. He kept saying there was no way I could have done that unless I was under the influence. I handed the policeman my travel mug of tea and told him he could check my tea if he wanted. The policeman shook me off and proceeded to shut the bald man up. The policeman told him to leave because I was just a scared kid and he was being unreasonable. As the policeman finished his paperwork, he turned to my dad and said, "Mr. Ziolko, you haven't said much. Is there anything you wanna say?"

Then my dad finally spoke up. "I told you not to wear those faggy flip-flops when you drive."

I tell the story, because there it was again, that word. "Why must he insist on relating me to this word?" I kept thinking. I failed again. I was so far removed from being a man that even my footwear was gay. I know it doesn't seem like that huge of a deal, but to have a father say those things to his son has more effect than you may be led to believe. After two really solid musical performances the evenings before the accident, I was looking for him to tell me how proud he was of me and instead, my manhood was questioned again.

This sent me into a spiral of confusion. After the incident, I went into a private stage of my life, where I actually thought I was gay. I had to have been. The only thing I knew about being a man was what I saw in my dad. Obviously I didn't turn out like him, and he didn't approve of how I turned out. Therefore, in my mind, the only other option was to be gay. It was a short time, and I want to clarify that I didn't act on anything, but the thoughts were damaging. I worked with several guys at my part-time job that lived this lifestyle, and I consulted them often, and they quickly embraced me and accepted me as a person. I liked the attention. I could talk fashion with them, and I could honestly be myself. It was through that, that I realized that I was certainly not gay, but liked their conversations. Plus, as a teenager, I blushed when I saw boobs.

I'm not fat, I'm just a man with boobs

This idea of being manly was something that I have battled since I was a kid. The boys were always bigger than me, stronger than me, faster than me, better at video games than me. You name it, the things that defined "masculinity" in our culture, they were better at it. I've struggled with identity and self-worth for as long as I can remember. And it only got harder as I got older. I thought after I got married, my self-worth would increase since I found someone who loved me for who I was. Well, that didn't happen.

We were on a cruise for our one year wedding anniversary, and that's when it hit me the hardest. I kept looking around and every ten seconds, I would see a guy who was in better shape than me or better looking than me. I felt like the scum on the bottom of the ship. I took my shirt off once for about ten minutes, the entire cruise. I just couldn't get myself to do it. There were too many people, too many judges, and I had too many flaws. Trust me, I'm aware at the level of concern for my insecurities and I am constantly working on them, but at that point, taking my shirt off was a risk. A risk I wasn't willing to take.

My perspective was unhealthy to say the least, but I am going to share my thought process with you while on the cruise. At that point in my life, it had been about four years since my dad left us, and I thought that if my own dad didn't love me, then how could anyone else—which led into this next part.

My wife, Ashley, is amazing. She tells me constantly how much she loves me and how much she doesn't care about the superficial things. However, the things pertaining to my self-esteem that related directly to issues with my dad overtook me, and Satan had a field day with it. I thought if I couldn't even get my dad to be proud of me and to stay in my life, then how could I guarantee that once I took off my shirt, my wife wouldn't run away? There was a buffet of delicious guys and I was the piece with too much fat that no one wants. It's ludicrous to think, but actually what I thought.

I struggled with my dad's acceptance most of my life, and when my parents got a divorce, it was the final blow. I couldn't help but think some part of it had to do with the disappointment in his only son. I mean, we are complete opposites. We don't even like the same football team. But seriously, who likes the New York Jets!?

———————

I have been struggling the past few years with my weight. I'm not fat or anything, but I am not anything close to skinny. I want to be skinny. I want to be tall and thin and wear skinny jeans that stop at my ankles. But instead, I'm fairly short with broad shoulders, a huge chest, thick quads, and the most ghetto booty you will ever see on a guy. Genetics stink. I'm the type of guy that if I work out, I just get bigger with muscle, but if I don't work out, I just get flabby. There is no in-between for me. People say I'm just not doing enough cardio, but that's false. The reality is, I'm not fat. My body type just isn't appealing to society's standards. I see it when I look in the mirror. I see broad shoulders, a lot of definition in my chest and back. I just have the body builder figure. Since my dad was a body builder, I guess it makes sense. But this is where the tension arises. Since I have a similar body structure as my dad, I look in the mirror and see the guy I failed to be.

I haven't revealed this to anyone, including my wife, but on days that I used to be home alone, I would sometimes see myself in the mirror and start to cry. I would see my dad, but inside, I knew I wasn't the man he wanted. I failed him. A man who would rather dance and sing on stage rather than play sports.

I stopped lifting serious weights when I was about twenty-one years old, two or three years after my dad left us. I would beat myself up about how lazy and inconsistent I was at it. But if I was honest with myself, I stopped lifting because it reminded me too much of what I was not and what I was missing.

The year before my dad left, he would come home from working the night shift and wake me up at 6 o'clock in the morning to go lifting. I got up almost everyday he would wake me up. This time, I wasn't sitting behind a counter watching. This time, he was spotting me as I bench pressed. It was me, my dad, and few of his gruff friends at the gym pumping iron. At one point on the car ride home, we were discussing my achievement of bench pressing over two hundred pounds, and he told me he was proud of me. Honestly, lifting was hard for me. Lifting by myself with my iPod isn't even close to what lifting was like with my dad. When I didn't have my dad to lift with anymore, the emotion was too much for me that I stopped going and defined my attitude on weight lifting based off of what I had lost with my dad.

We all have wounds

When I look back at my life story thus far, I realize that my story is not that unique. There are too many kids with too many wounds and so many kids living in anger and confusion. So many stories of pain and struggle with self-esteem and allowing society to tell them what is acceptable and what isn't; allowing society to dictate what is beautiful and what is insignificant.

The problem is that we all suffer wounds. When I look at society, I see wound after wound; yet, I see few scars. Unfortunately, many of us never really heal from our wounds, and I think it's because we don't know how to heal or are afraid of how the wounds will affect us if we heal. But who says these wounds have to affect us negatively?

My experiences have helped shape me into the person I am today, but It wasn't just the trials themselves that got me to where I am. It was when I decided to stop re-opening the wounds and allow God to heal them. Through my experiences, I was able to seek God and what His plans for life, marriage, and acceptance are. I don't have to follow the past.

The beauty in all of this is: *we don't have to find our identities in our wounds*. We have all been dealt a bad hand of cards at some point. But do we define the whole card game based on a bad hand or two? We can't. Otherwise we'll lose the game, and that's not what God intends. We don't need to find our identities in our wounds, we need to find our identities in Christ who can heal them. Once we allow Christ to bring us healing, they are not a part of our identity but merely a scar that will fade over time. That's when true reconciliation of self will begin.

REFILL OR OVERFLOW

Polack Hill

I used to live on a hill in Pennsylvania. This hill was nick-named "Polack Hill" because of the overwhelming presence of Polish people and sauerkraut. On this little hill, in my tiny home-town, there were five Catholic churches, two Polish taverns, and a city wide "Polish Festival" held every year. They would commandeer the parking lot of one of the Catholic churches and set up a bunch of tents. Then people would flock to this Catholic church parking lot under giant tents eating pierogies and sauer-kraut with adults drinking at the beer tent. Yes, adults crowded a beer tent next to a church. Kids would play in a tent dedicated to games while the old people sat in front of a portable stage listening to accordion-led music. It was quite the complex.

All my neighbors were really old and had distinctive polish last names. Names like Kulbaski, Kaninski and Zebieg. One of my old neighbors, Leo, had his driveway in our backyard. It was a long driveway that led up to a large open carport. As a child I always imagined the carport as a sweet fort for me and friends. Leo loved warm summer days. He would sit in a lawn chair at the entry point to where the driveway met the carport wearing no shirt, drinking beer, and blasting polka music with even more accordions. He always made jokes about my Italian heritage and, as I got older, I realized that a lot of them were inappropriate.

Everyone in my neighborhood had real, outdoor clothes lines and never seemed to use an actual clothes dryer. There were no fences, and all the yards and houses blended together into an interesting community. But it was a community that was real and friendly.

Polack Hill was a great place to live and grow up, but was a bad place to live when the weather got bad or when your car was low on gas.

I remember one specific time growing up on Polack Hill when I hadn't even had my drivers license for a year. It was around that time as a teenager where you have that disturbing revelation that you actually have to fill up your car with gas. All the years prior, you would watch your parents stop at gas stations, but you thought gas stations were just the place you went when you wanted travel size Funions and slushies.

It was a brisk morning and just cold enough to make the pipelines in my car cold. If you don't know anything about cars and pipes like me, and live where it gets cold, you quickly learn that if your gas tank is not full enough, your gas lines can freeze.

On this particular morning, it wasn't quite cold enough to freeze them but cold enough that when I triggered the ignition, the car made a *ka-ka-ka-ka* sound that even for me, the idiot of cars, could recognize as a bad sound. I tried again . . . and again . . . and again getting the same results. It was then it dawned on me I hadn't filled my car with gas in a while, and I remembered seeing that orange gas pump symbol light up the night before. Panicking I wouldn't be able to make it to school, I tried one last time. This time the car fired up. Hesitantly it fired up, but it fired up nonetheless.

I glanced at the gas meter and the gas was so low the needle was pointing below the giant E line. At this point, the car was making a putting sound, and it was clear to me the car was running merely on fumes. *I just got to get to the gas station by Palumbo's Meat Market*, I thought.

Now let me explain the geographic location of this gas station to you. My house sat in a neighborhood atop Polack Hill. This gas station sat a top a smaller hill just below us. Now it would have been great if there was just a downhill road that led to this gas station. But for reasons I do not understand, the only way to access this gas station was to head slightly downhill on one road, make a right onto another road which took a steep plunge downhill like a roller-coaster and then back up a steep incline. Once atop the crest of this hill, the road slanted downhill slightly a few hundred feet to a traffic light. The gas station was just across the street of the traffic light. The only way to go downhill was to go uphill.

So when I said to myself, *I just got to get to the gas station by Palumbo's Meat Market*, I wasn't just cruising down the street real quick to the next corner. I knew I was about to embark on a journey. A journey that would be merely a flip of the coin as to whether I would make it or not.

Also, I should mention at this time I wasn't the muscular, sexy specimen I am now. I was skinny and probably hadn't even hit puberty yet. Which meant if I got stranded, I was not going to be able to push my car anywhere. I didn't have a cell phone, it was too cold to walk anywhere, and I was too afraid to hitch-hike.

I shifted my car into gear and began my journey. I made the right turn to the steep hill and my stomach tensed up like it does at the top of the track on a roller-coaster. I then began my decent, accelerating quickly. Then about half way down the hill, I hear my car shut off. Yes, it shut off. I had run out of gas. Instinctively, I popped my car into neutral. I took a deep breath and hoped to gain enough speed to make it up the steep incline. I hit the bottom of the hill and jolted quickly uphill. The closer to the top I got, the slower my car went.

I barely made it to top of the hill, as I finally took a breath. However I wasn't done. I still had to make it a few hundred more feet and through a traffic light. It took a few seconds for the car to gain a little momentum, but I began my slight decent to the traffic light. *What if the light was red and I have to stop*, I thought? Coasting at a tremendous speed around eight miles per hour, I approached the traffic light and it was red. I closed my eyes for just a second and hoped it would turn green. And just as I was almost right underneath the traffic light, it turned green. I graciously coasted across the street to the gas station and filled up.

You would think I would have learned my lesson to never let my tank get that low again. False. I run it low consistently, except now that I'm older, I'm not afraid to hitch-hike.

All that for a game?!

Sports leagues and fans are interesting to me. One Sunday evening, my wife and I were watching an NFL football game on the television when she made an interesting observation. It's an observation that I already know and am aware of, but sometimes forget the magnitude of it.

She proceeded to explain how perplexing it was to her how much time, money, and attention goes into one single playoff game. There were former professional football players hired as analysts as they sat in a massively produced television studio, in expensive suits talking about all aspects of the game, the players, and even the stadium. The amount of money spent on producing that thirty minute pre-game show had to be in the millions, and the hours spent producing it had to be off the charts.

Then we tuned into the game. The amount of money spent on the game was astronomical. Let's start with tickets and parking. The average stadium holds around seventy-five thousand screaming fans. Fans pay a minimum, typically, of about sixty dollars per ticket for the worst seats in the stadium and as much as thousands of dollars for the best, most luxurious seats in the stadium. I recently went to a professional football game, and I was shocked at the prices of parking. My friend and I parked a half-mile from the stadium, and parking was still forty dollars for the game. Everyone had team jerseys on, which on average cost around one hundred dollars.

Now consider the amount of money spent of food. In the NFL, the average hotdog, pretzel, etc. ranges from six to ten dollars, not to mention the average of ten dollars per drink for alcohol. Consider the amount of money spent on paying the employees of the stadium to keep things running smoothly. Think about the electric, water, and gas bill for the stadium. What about the amount of money spent on maintenance?

After all of that, we have to now think about the money spent on endorsements and advertisements. All the banners, ads, and "sponsored by's" cost money: a lot of money. What about the television commercials? And don't forget about the wonderful salaries of the main office staff, the entire coaching staff, the officials, training staff, medical staff, security staff, and of course the players. This isn't even all of the money spent, but it has to easily creep into the billions. And the time spent on this one game is easily in the hundreds of hours.

All of this for a game. A silly game.

And while the game commences, the fans, in all their glory, respond to prompts, chants, and songs. Some fans wear face paint with their jerseys and some like to add flare to their jerseys essentially creating a super-fan costume. Chances are good that you don't know any of the people around you, yet when a play goes well for your team, you find yourself hugging and high-fiving them all while losing your voice screaming and cheering for them.

At the same time my wife and I are discussing this, I began

to cheer and scream at the television in excitement as the team I was cheering for pulled ahead.

The question posed that night was *why?* Why do we get so excited for a game? Why do we spend so much energy on a game, when it will end, and we will likely forget about it a year later?

The answer is because *we were made to worship.* We were created with emotions and endorphins so we can express our worship to the best of our human abilities.

The problem is we have chosen to worship the wrong things. Sports and competitions consume us because it gives us the opportunity to believe in something, someone.

Football is more fun than church

It's Sunday morning before the big game, and Alex's alarm goes off. He's frustrated because he only gets the weekend to sleep-in and he has to get up early to go to church. He rolls over, hits his wife with his still sleeping arm and asks her if they really have to go to church today. She says yes, and he knows he should because they skipped last week already.

By the time Alex actually convinces himself to roll out of bed, he's already behind schedule. He still has to shower and get the kids ready. His morning is full of chaos as he hops from one room to another trying to get everyone ready. By the time he gets the youngest dressed, their middle child has already thrown their bowl of cereal on the floor, and as he tries to clean it up, his youngest decides they want to open the cabinets and pull all the pots and pans out. After yelling at everyone, he finally gets everyone corralled into the van even more behind schedule.

Alex rolls into the church parking lot and his blood pressure starts to boil. Their kids are arguing with each other, and he can't find a parking spot.

"You would think they would have more parking. This is ridiculous," he says to his wife neglecting the fact that there is no parking left because he was ten minutes late. If he would have been ten minutes early, he would have found a spot.

By the time Alex and his wife get the kids checked-in to the children's areas, they finally stumble into the auditorium only to find themselves in the same situation as the parking lot. No empty seats available by themselves without having to actually sit beside some people.

After finding a seat next to people, he tunes his attention to the stage as they begin their last song of the music set. He's annoyed because he only gets to sing one song and it's not even one he knows, and the guy who is charge of the lyrics on the screen is constantly putting the words on the screen late. *How can I worship when I can't even know the song or even have the words at the right time*, he thinks to himself.

During the greeting time, he quickly pulls out his phone, so people won't approach him, scanning email, Twitter, Facebook, and Instagram. Then about thirty minutes into the pastor's sermon, he begins to get antsy hoping he is going to wrap it up soon. When the pastor does actually finish, he beelines to the door because they need to get home to prepare for the football party at their house later that night.

On the drive home, his wife asks the kids what they learned and they respond with a flood of answers about how boring it was. Alex sort of nods his head, thinking the same thing. Meanwhile, all Alex can remember from the service was that the band only played songs he didn't know, the slide guy was late with the words on the screen, and the pastor spoke a little too long. Also, the person next him had on the worst smelling perfume.

Alex pulls in the driveway and a sudden ease comes over him. He smiles as he thinks about the party he is going to have and the game he has been waiting for all week. Alex watched all the interviews, compared stats, and talked about it with everyone he knew discussing which team was better. Now he gets to watch the pre-game and relax all day.

Running our tanks on empty

I like to blame the fact I run the gas tank on my car so low on my parents. The years leading up to getting my license, I watched my parents. I saw how they did things with the car. In fact a common phrase in my household was, "I need to get gas, the car's on E." While it may seem like an excuse, it is true. My entire life, I watched my parents run the gas tank on the car very low before filling it up. So of course, when I got my license, what did I think to be true about filling up your gas tank? You wait until you're on E.

What Alex doesn't realize is he is instilling in his children an attitude about God and church. Alex doesn't get excited to go to church and worship God, if he even worships at all. The music is annoying to him, the preaching is too long, and he'd rather be somewhere else. So it's no surprise then, his children feel the same way. What Alex is teaching his children about church is the same thing my parents unintentionally taught me about filling up my car with gas: "I need to fill up, I'm on E."

This is where the problem arises. We are continuing to raise generations that only go to church because their tanks are empty and they need to fill up. We treat church like a gas station. We come, fill up, grab some tasty treats, complain when the soda machine is out of order, and don't look back until we are running on fumes a week or so later.

This is where the church crumbles. Look at American churches today. It is a similar image to the gas station that has the lowest price on a gallon of gas. Cars are lined up trying to fill their tanks before the prices rise again. The church is full of people trying to fill up. What happens when all these masses of people show up, trying to fill their tanks? The church runs out of resources. Before you know it, we are complaining because there are not enough women's programs, the coffee tastes bad, the seats aren't comfortable enough, the band plays too many new songs, the band plays the same songs too much, the pastor preaches too long, not to mention he never has time for us. He is our pastor and our tithes pay for his salary. He should be at our beck and call. No one said hi to us even though we didn't make an effort on our own to talk to anyone. And even worse, we will blame the fact we didn't engage in worship on the church and its staff. If they would have done a better job with the music and lights, I would have felt it more. If the pastor's sermon had more energy and jokes, I wouldn't have gotten bored and would have actually learned something.

All of a sudden it's like our churches' soda machines are out of order and that annoys us. So what do we do? We go to another gas station. And we'll go there until they disappoint us.

We are a generation of gas station church goers who run our tanks so low that we are running on fumes before we ever go back.

Is that what church is supposed to be? What if church wasn't about us? What if church was a privilege and an honor to go to? What if we went to church simply to respond to God in worship and praise Him for being holy because we are not? What if church was our overflow? A church full of people already filled up with the Holy Spirit from the week, that Sunday is a place to release our overflow?

We are overflowing in the wrong things. Instead of living Christ-centered lives, we live lives centered around sports statistics, interviews, television shows, shopping, restaurants, etc. We give God a little bit of time—if any at all—and, most of the time, it's a hassle.

To overflow means to wake up in the morning, giving God your first thoughts and even words. Ask Him to fill you with His grace and love, and continue that all throughout the day. Every person you talk to, every choice you make, everything you do, you do it as an act of worship to God. As if you are presenting that conversation to God as worship. And you don't just do it *for* God, but *because* of God.

Then on Sunday, there is no annoyance. There is no stress. You excitedly wake up early and get to church early because you simply cannot wait to give God your worship once again.

I'm a pastor, and even I'm terrible at this. I spend my weeks preparing for services and meeting with people from the church, and there will be days that go by and I have been doing so many work projects *for* God but not *because* of God. I do them for God but because of *me*. Because I want to do projects that make the people happy so they think I'm doing a good job and leadership won't fire me. I do it because I want the affirmation that I am a good worker.

We are human, so it's impossible to do this perfectly, but what if that was our daily pursuit? The weeks I am consistent with this, my life is filled with no stress, a closer relationship with my Savior, and my work is totally different. So different, it's noticeable—at least for me.

God Wants It All; Including You

One of the important things I learned about running my gas tank low consistently was it is actually bad for your vehicle. I've got quite the schooling on cars, so you can trust me. I know a lot. I spent an hour reading about them on Wikipedia.

When you run your tank low all the time, you are actually allowing air in your gas tank. With air in the tank, that creates moisture and moisture creates condensation. This creates rust. Do this enough and your gas tank will rust out. When we treat church as a gas station, and run our faith tanks low, we let air in our faith tanks and the enemy loves that. The air in our faith tanks vary from person to person. Sometimes air is sports, vanity, shopping, television . . . the list goes on. But eventually that air will cause rust, damaging our faith.

God's wants all of us all the time, but He does this not because He needs it. God doesn't need worship. God is still just as powerful and majestic whether we worship Him or not. He wants us to worship Him, because He knows when we fill our tanks with Him and not air, it will keep us healthy and our tanks won't rust when they're full.

OCD

I hate flying in airplanes. I'm not sure if it's because of the
incredibly comfortable and spacious seats, the giant portions of
Ritz cheddar crackers, the forty-five minute stalls on the tarmac,
or the combination of two hundred people crammed together
with no air flow and stale farts. Who doesn't like standing in a
security line for thirty minutes just to wait at your terminal for
another hour, only to sit next to the old guy with no friends who
wants to tell you about his eleven grandchildren, leaving you the
only other alternative but to put on headphones and be stuck
watching a Nicholas Cage film the plane is offering? Sounds
like it's worth every penny of the zillion-dollar plane ticket that
will deplete my bank account. But really, the main reason I hate
flying is because I'm not in control of the situation and I hate it
when I'm not in control, especially with something like my life on
the line.

I was flying a while back, and about two hours into the flight I was getting a little antsy. And since I refuse to pee on airplanes, I needed something to do to occupy my mind until I landed. And don't judge me. You think guys have bad aim with toilets on the ground? Try to imagine a man peeing high in the air with the bathroom shaking. And since I usually travel in flip-flops . . . I'm not taking that risk. No thank you. So, I decided to lean out into the isle and assess the situation around me. Honestly, I wanted to see if anyone was snoring or doing something funny that I could entertain myself with.

I began eaves dropping on the financial report the gentleman across the aisle in front of me was working on. For the record, if you're going to do a financial report, you should probably learn how to use Microsoft Excel first. Otherwise, you are just providing free entertainment to the creepy guy who has to pee behind you. But that's when the unthinkable happened.

Out of my peripheral, I saw movement up front. I looked up front and exiting the cockpit was the pilot. He headed toward the restroom. That's when the thought crossed my mind, *Um . . . who is flying the plane?* I hunched forward as my senses heightened, and I began to frantically look around. Naturally, I was expecting the plane to begin to do a nosedive. After the pilot exited the restroom, I engaged in a sigh of relief and leaned back into my seat. I watched the pilot make his way back to the cockpit only to stop just short of the door to keep my suspense in full throttle. What did this pilot do? He slouched on the little counter space in the front of the plane with a cup of coffee and chatted away with the flight attendant. Leaning forward again, I felt my heart rate begin to rise. This time, with a little more intensity, my mind shouted, *Who is flying the plane?!*

Auto-pilot is the darnedest thing. The pilot can set the co-ordinates, and boom, the plane is flying itself. They can just kick back, relax, enjoy the ride, and apparently find out if the flight attendant has a boyfriend. Let me tell you what I wanted to do on this flight. Rush the cockpit like a teenager rushes the stage at a Justin Bieber concert and take over the controls, cussing profusely at the pilot for being terrible at his job. The fact the pilot wasn't in the cockpit really drove me crazy. For my own sense of security, I wanted him in his cockpit seat, at least pretending to fly the plane. That's how I envisioned it in my head, so therefore, that's how it was supposed happen. I wanted to take control of the plane just to make sure we wouldn't crash. But we all know how that would end.

Personal space

One weird thing about me is my personal space. I don't have a problem with clutter or messes anywhere unless it's my personal space. I can visit someone who is living in absolute filth and clearly qualifying for the show *Hoarders* and not be affected by it at all. In fact, I embrace it. It's their space. They can use cardboard boxes filled with their collection of G.I. Joes as an eating table. I don't care. They don't have to buy food for their cats because of the decomposing rats under the trash that they refuse to take to the dumpster. Bravo!

But come into my personal space, move a beverage coaster on my coffee table in my living room a half-inch and I will stab you. Go ahead, test me. Everything has its place—and it needs to stay there. I'm surprised I barely passed Geometry because in my personal space, I'm the master of angles and spaces.

One day I was adjusting the ottoman in our living room, because it wasn't exactly lined up perfectly and spaced perfectly between the love-seat and the couch. So I did what any insane person would do. I walked up to the ottoman positioning myself square with the piece of furniture. I closed my left eye to create the best "eye-level" and slowly began walking backwards. I did this until the long edge of the top cushion of the ottoman lined up perfectly with the bottom edge of the frame of the couch. If it wasn't flush, I would adjust it mere centimeters at a time and repeat the process until the ottoman was flush with the edge of the couch frame.

During this process of mine one day, I walked backwards right into my wife. Whom was standing behind me with her arms crossed, clearly judging me, and probably laughing inside. *"What in the world are you attempting to do?"* she asked in a tone which conveyed that she certainly feared the possible range of answers.

"I'm making the ottoman flush with the couch," I declared with confidence. Because in my mind, it made perfect sense. That's what you do to make furniture flush and square.

"By walking backwards?" she questioned.

"Well yah, but I'm closing my left eye," I defended.

She looked even more confused than the beginning as she responded, "What?!"

"Well, I close my left eye and . . . uh [sigh] . . . I mean I line up the edge of the top cushion of the ottoman with the bottom thing of the couch and . . . well [another sigh] . . . never mind. You won't understand." I concluded my scientific explanation in defeat.

"You're crazy!" she said as she turned and walked away shaking her head.

Having all my furniture and decorations in a position I want, makes me feel safe. It's the thing about me people laugh about the most: declaring the insanity level of my Obsessive Compulsive-Disorder (OCD). Except for the few people who helped me move apartments several years back and saw the organization level of my underwear drawer. They hold me at another level of insanity. On my kitchen counter, all my appliances have a place, an angle, and they need to stay there. If my coffee pot is shifted from the perfect angle I've selected for it, I need to fix it or I'll have an aneurysm. Logically, those are my only two options.

Well, there was a season of life that was extremely difficult for me. I had just moved halfway across the country, left all family and friends, and moved to a town in which I knew no one. Then I started a new job at a church, and we all know how much congregation members love change. We also moved into a house we purchased with a significantly difficult process. On top of that, my wife was very pregnant and about to pop. Add the stress of becoming a new father on top of all that life change, and it's the perfect recipe for my OCD to produce an impressive level of anxiety. And that's exactly what happened.

The baby came and, for help and support, we had both sets of families come stay at our house. It was my in-laws, my parents, my sister, and brother in-law. That's eight adults and one newborn in one house! Look in the dictionary for the definition of insanity and that is it.

Two days after we left the hospital with our beautiful baby girl, we had to go do a check up with the doctor. The wife and I packed up our daughter in the car seat like we were packing up drinking glasses to move across the country. We even considered using bubble wrap on the car seat. We went to the doctors and were back home within an hour. I walked in the door to find that all my furniture in my living room had been rearranged. My mom thought it would be a great idea to rearrange all our living room furniture. We weren't even gone a full hour! Now, you have to understand, this is absolutely normal behavior for my mother. My mother is a creative artist, who is a great interior designer, so you would think I would expect that from her.

Instead, I walked in, saw the change, and had the meltdown of the year. I felt this overwhelming feeling of nausea overcome me. I wanted to throw up and felt a little dizzy. The one place I found my security and comfort was in shambles, and I was already feeling overwhelmed with lack of sleep. I found my way to the couch, feeling sick, and the meltdown commenced. Feeling paralyzed from the change, I began to cry. I didn't like the change and emotionally could not handle it. Things were not the way I wanted them and where I wanted them. My mother sat on the couch next me and consoled my anxiety attack. "What's wrong dear? Are you okay? I just moved the couches to maximize your living room space."

I had a hard time accepting the change. I had become comfortable with the environment my furniture was in and now it was ruined. Of course, like usual, a few days later I realized how much better the positioning of the furniture was and quickly became fond of it. Now that positioning of the furniture is my safety and comfort. If someone were to move it now, I would more than likely cry again.

It's stories like that I look back on and assess as a major control issue. The reason I had a meltdown was not because I liked the couch better in the old spot. It's the couch was moved and changed without my planning, preparation, and intention of moving it myself. The situation was out of my control and I didn't like that.

Tony Land

My wife always tells me that I live in Tony Land. I like that concept because I like to think Tony Land would be an awesome place. I would serve Dippin' Dots ice cream for free, and I would love to see a mascot of myself running around the park. There would also be a giant water slide.

My wife tells me how idealistic I really am. It's true. I like to credit that to my mother. I credit my mother for her ability to create an experience out of anything. Christmas mornings as a child were so magical. I'm pretty sure part of the reason was because we didn't have much money growing up, so my mom did everything she could to make the morning special and meaningful to help mask the fact that we didn't get a ton of gifts. It was like walking downstairs to a winter wonderland. Because she is so creative, she has strong visions in her head about how things should go or happen. And we all know how things in our heads are. Perfect and ideal. They are massive and usually unrealistic. This is one quality I received from my mother. I am very idealistic. I have strong visions of what I want things to look like, and I expect things to go that way. And when things don't go the way I envision them in my head or if the people don't meet the expectations I feel like needs to happen to execute my perfect plans, I get really frustrated and stressed.

The truth is I want things to be perfect. I expect things to be perfect, and I expect people to perform with perfection. This is why I love planning. I love to plan out my visions to go perfectly. And by perfectly, I mean how I want them to go. And inevitably, something will happen that will cause a slight adjustment. I don't like adjustments. I like perfection.

In fact, even the process of writing this book—*which was a four-year process*—is proof of that. When I first got the idea to write a book and started the process, I was excited. I had all these visions on how the process would go. Let me explain them to you. I planned I would sit down twice a week in a Starbucks, wearing my coolest clothes. I wanted to look important and feel important. They always say dress for the job you want, not the job you have. I would put on my coolest shirt, my coolest shoes and order a hipster cup of coffee. I would sit down next to the window looking out upon the pretty grass, put my headphones on, and start typing. Then people would come in and see me typing in my cool clothes and assume I was important. I would bust out a chapter in a few hours, and then when I finished a chapter that was perfect with even the first draft, I would go home feeling accomplished. Well, here's what really happened.

My coolest shirt didn't fit because I gained weight; so I had to wear a not-so-cool one. When I got to Starbucks, the line was out the door and there were no tables open. I finally ordered my coffee and managed to snag a table by the window. I was back on track, until I took and sip and realized they didn't make my drink right. When I sat down, the table was significantly smaller than I expected and it made it difficult for me to fit my laptop, coffee, and wireless mouse. I was also out of reach of an outlet, and I would need to charge my laptop soon. When I opened my laptop, I looked out the window to the beautiful scenery; which was actually a parking lot to Trader Joe's. There was a glare on my screen from the sun causing me to not be able to see my screen well, so I had to close the blinds. The temperature was freezing inside the store, so I battled hypothermia.

After combating all the challenges, I typed "Here are a few things to consider while reading" and got ready to dominate my first chapter. As I typed my first chapter, I hit a creative block, so I decided to check Facebook. I checked in on ex-girlfriends, old classmates and saw a post that told me if I didn't share the photo of the cross, I didn't really love Jesus. I didn't finish the chapter, and apparently I don't love Jesus.

After I actually finished the first chapter and few others, I felt really accomplished. I was proud of myself. So I decided to give it to a few friends to read and edit them. I told them to edit away, but deep in my heart, I knew that they were going to hand it back to me and say, "It's perfect! It's the best chapter I've ever read! I didn't have to change anything because it was so perfect and amazing!"

After they all read the chapters, they gave me the chapters back with their feedback. I think the paper had more red marker on it than black ink. One lady actually had me visit her in her office and told me it was bad. The paper was well-written, but simply not that good because of the message I was conveying and how I was conveying it. Talk about shattered glass that was my self-esteem.

I changed all the chapters and felt even better, so I wrote five more. Then I woke up one morning, hated every chapter and every sentence I had written. I was angry because of how bad my writing was. *No one's going to read this.* I said to myself. I deleted all seven chapters. Now I'm neck deep into re-writing what I've been trying to say for years, a lot better. However, at the particular time that I'm writing this exact chapter, I am now a father with a more demanding ministry job. That means I get very small amounts of time to work on chapters in between picking up Cheerios from the floor, dreaming about Baby Einstein puppets, and the easy task of managing volunteers at church. All of which has set my goal for finishing the book back about two years. Needless to say, my ideal situation for writing a book has turned into a hodgepodge of scenarios that involve me getting a few minutes to slap something onto paper and just hope it isn't awful. Thank God for Beats headphones.

Building snowmen

I've never really had a knack for building snowmen. When I do build a snowman, I usually receive compliments about how good my child's snowman is. Then I have to break the news to them I don't have a child old enough to make a snowman and that I actually built it myself. It surprises me I'm not good at building snowmen, because I am a champion at making snowballs. So much so, that my wife's nickname for me is "The Snowballer." However, it typically means I like to *snowball* a situation, not make actual snowballs. And for me, when I snowball a situation, it always ends with someone dying.

If you want to see my snowballing skills, just involve me in money matters. In our household, my wife handles all our money. I don't know how much money we have, and more importantly, how much money we don't have. Sometimes, I will call my wife and ask her how much money I can use to fill up the car with gas. I don't need to know the bank account info and at this point, I don't want to. It's not that I'm irresponsible with money. It's just when I think about money, my anxiety skyrockets, I freak out, snowball the situation until it ends with us all dead. And that's exhausting.

After a few months of being married, I was determined to be the man of the house and appoint myself household Chief Financial Officer. Except there was just one problem with that: I was terrible at it. I managed to find the longest, most complicated and stressful way to do the finances. One month, while I was cussing at the computer screen and pulling my hair out, my wife decided to take over. She is efficient, calm, and of course, good at it. I was determined to do things my way because I was assured my way was the best way to do it; even if it was the longest, most complicated, and ridiculous. I had a hard time giving up control of that feature of our lives. I wanted to control the money and the process involved with our finances.

One of the reasons I get so stressed with money is because I realize just how close to being homeless we really are. Okay, maybe not really homeless, but the fact that our lives may seem stable are actually really fragile and can turn quickly.

When I begin to snowball, my wife will sometimes indulge

my process just to walk me through my insanity. When we are done, I usually see how ridiculous I sound. Here's how a normal snowball situation would work for me.

Hitting my hand from away from my mouth, my wife asked, "Tony, what's wrong? You're biting you're nails, which means your anxious."

"It's just . . . I don't know."

"Well, you do know, so tell me," she commanded.

Staggeringly I replied, "I don't know, I guess . . . it's just like one thing after another. We finally paid off our debt and now this? It's like God just wants us in debt, and we don't even have cable!"

"Well, I understand, but we'll be fine. Has God ever not provided?" I slightly tilt my head to the right and raise my left upper lip as she continued. "That's what I thought. You always get anxious with stuff like this and you know He'll provide. So why are you so anxious?"

I sighed. "I'm just afraid, because what if we never get out of debt, and then I lose my job. Then we can't pay our debt and bills. Then we couldn't pay for our house, so they'd kick us out. And then we'd have to live on the street. And because I wouldn't have a job, I would fail even more as a provider and couldn't feed my family. So we'd all starve."

"Then what?" she said, only provoking my snowball.

With panic in my voice I say, "Well, we'd die Ashley, we'd die."

"Right, because we have one additional fairly large hospital bill, that means we're gonna die. That makes sense." she sarcastically indulged my thought process.

Now obviously, that's the most logical progression of events. The point of this, though, is to emphasize even more of my control issues. It's not that I actually think we will be homeless and die. The reality is we could always move in with family. The main issue is I don't like the unknown. It tends to be less of the outcome and more of the inability to know what's going to happen. So when I would do a budget, I had to make sure every penny was accounted for. And if one penny was out of line, or a bill fluctuated in taxes, I would freak out.

Perfection or control?

I think there's a misconception about people who have OCD. Most people associate this with just being a perfectionist: wanting things to be neat, orderly, and have to have all the labels of your pantry cans facing the same way. But it's so much more than that. OCD is a control issue. It's all about control. You can be messy and have OCD. At the core, people who struggle with OCD have a hard time with the lack of control over situations. We need to do things our way, even if it's the more difficult way.

Being able to control situations is what we thrive on. Therefore, my calendar is my best friend. I live and die by it. Everything I do is on that calendar. Nothing throws me in a tizzy more than when I have a meeting scheduled and it gets moved or cancelled. It will literally ruin my day.

At my current job, we used to have staff meetings every Thursday at nine o'clock in the morning. One Thursday, my wife was dropping me off at work for staff meeting and I noticed our lead pastor's car wasn't in his normal parking spot. It was quickly approaching nine in the morning and he wasn't at the church. I started to panic. *It's staff meeting day. Where's Dave!? It's Thursday morning. That's staff meeting day.* Then, just before the clock struck nine, I received a text. He informed the staff that something came up, and he had to cancel staff meeting. I looked at my calendar to see if maybe it was a different day. It was still Thursday. I said to myself, *But it's Thursday morning. And Thursday morning is staff meeting day. He knows that. Every Thursday at nine in the morning, we have staff meeting. Because my calendar says that today is staff meeting from nine until ten. Like, that's what were supposed to be doing. What am I going to do?*

I kid you not, I honestly sat in my office from nine until ten and didn't do anything. I didn't know what to do. Because in my mind, and in my calendar, it said I needed to have staff meeting from nine until ten.

We all have those times in life. Those times in life that feel like we are in limbo and seem to have no control. Those times in life when you just want control, because you fear the idea of not knowing what's going to happen. Maybe it's that job you no longer have. Maybe it's that dream you have, but you're afraid to take the leap to pursue it. Maybe you and your spouse want kids, but you're afraid how it will mess up your lives—trust me, they will! Maybe it's that disease that has you scared to death. Or maybe your spouse just up and left.

Those are all situations that have us all saying, "Who's flying the plane?" In those moments we don't know what's happening or who's flying the plane, we do what comes natural to us. Our senses heighten and fear overcomes us. We rush to the cock-pit, take the controls, and attempt to fly the plane ourselves. The only problem with this is that most of us don't know how to fly planes. Since we don't know what we're doing, we suffer from stress, anxiety, and even more crippling fear.

You have to trust the auto-pilot. When it comes to our lives and our faith, we have to realize that we either don't know how to fly a plane or can't do it as well as auto-pilot can. When life seems like no one is flying your plane, or you are doing a terrible job at it, just set your coordinates to God and enjoy the auto-pilot. Because the quicker we learn this, the quicker we learn that with God, our lives are on auto-pilot, the quicker it will make sense. Don't get me wrong; it will still be terrifying. But we need to realize that the auto-pilot will put us on the most direct and straight path to our set coordinates: our Savior. And putting your trust in that will be scary, but sit back, don't fret, and don't forget to rejoice in the fact that you are partaking in the wonderful and amazing act of *flying!*

WHY I SAY FANCY

I used to use the British word "fancy" all the time—and I've never even been to England. When I was attending University—another cool British term—my friends and I were hanging out in the school's student union when one of the prettiest girls I had ever seen up to that point in my life walked by. To clarify, my wife is now the prettiest girl I've ever seen. Did you hear that, Ashley? You are the prettiest girl I've ever seen! Like a typical nineteen year old, one of my friends mumbled with wide eyes, "Wow, she's hot!" then continued stuffing his mouth full of greasy chicken tenders.

Then with every ounce of primitive nature in his bones, another one of my friends piggy-backed the statement by jumping right in the conversation, "My, oh my, I would like to (insert perverted gesture)." Now imagine him terribly acting out that perverted gesture. On second thought, don't.

I ended the trifecta by adding, "I do fancy that gal."

"Are you gay?" Mr. Chicken Tenders disgustingly replied as he limped his wrist asserting even more he questioned my sexuality.

"No man. I was just saying how pretty she was." Of course I said that as I sipped my sugar-free, nonfat, no-whip latte. What? I was watching my figure. Trust me, I do like girls.

"Whatever dude," he ended. "You sound like a socialist. I'm just gonna pretend that never happened."

I sat there confused, not understanding what had happened. Was he calling me gay or a socialist? Or was he calling socialists gay? Conclusion: he was a nineteen-year-old college student with no filter. Chances were good he didn't even know himself and probably heard the word in a class and associated England with socialists.

It honestly never even occurred to me saying "fancy" sounded weird until they scolded me for talking like a socialist. Don't get me wrong, I love the United Kingdom and the idea of free medicine, but I also hate the idea of raising taxes. If taxes go up, my paychecks would be smaller, and that would make me sad. Plus, I'm from a town of less than eight thousand people located in the farms of Pennsylvania. You have to hate that kind of stuff living there, otherwise you run the risk of being chased down by a tractor. Now I know what you're thinking, "Tony, you could totally out run a tractor." I thought the same thing until I was put with the fat lineman to run sprints at football practice in ninth grade. At that point, you just accept the fact that you're slow. Plus, tractors have very large wheels.

Now, one of the reasons I said fancy instead of the American way was because I thought it made me sound sophisticated. When I said that word, I got enjoyment out of watching people look at me confused, as if I were complimenting their clothing.

When British people talk, I listen. Not because what they say is any more important, but because I just can't understand what the heck they are saying. Plus, their accent is wicked awesome. It's true. I once believed that President Obama was white just because a British person told me so. I then realized that he was cappuccino with a lot of sugar.

I started using the word fancy unknowingly from one of my friends, Jon. Before I continue, you should know something about him. He is originally from Canada, adopted by a Canadian Chinaman and a Canadian Swedish woman. He has another adopted brother who is Filipino. Sound like a good sitcom? I think so. His dad's job relocated the family from Canada to Southern California and then up to the farm towns of Pennsylvania. Jon is a socialist and I love it. He used to always get upset when I would say that, but I know that at heart, he is. He never really liked the American system. He would tell me all the time.

What I liked about Jon was how different he was from everyone else—and he didn't care. He was in his twenties, and he flaunted his obsession with video games, comic books, art, science fiction, old school punk, and most importantly, writing. We took a few writing classes together, hung out at wannabe diners, occasionally shared beers, talked about God, music, film, politics, and literature. The conversations were mostly one-sided as I pretended to understand what he was saying.

At one point, Jon jumped on a plane to England, studied abroad for half a year, and came back with a British girlfriend. Then, after he decided England was better than America, he jumped back on a plane and moved there. When he returned from his first trip to England, he started using all this British lingo, and I honestly thought he was weird. It wasn't long until I was unintentionally doing it.

What Jon didn't realize was how much he affected my relationship with God. My family went through a tragedy. He was one of the few friends who knew me before the tragedy and stuck it out with me through the whole thing. It meant a lot. A lot of my friends at the time bailed when I needed them most. Not Jon.

When times are tough, our characters are revealed. We start to reflect the lives of those we cling to. Their personality attributes start to rub off on us—unintentionally. I think this can happen in our walks with God.

Socialism, bars and God's attributes

As a Christian, I am called to live by the attributes of God. It's prevalent all throughout Scripture. One of the issues that I ran into personally, is I like to choose which attributes of Christ to reflect. It's funny because if I had my way, I would not have chosen the word fancy from Jon's vocabulary to reflect. But that's not how it works. Someone rubs off on you when you allow them and you open yourself up to become vulnerable. You spend gobs of time with them *because you want to*, and before you know it you are laughing like them. That's how it is with

Christ. I don't get choose which attributes of His fit my lifestyle. It's simply a bi-product of spending time with God. It's unintentional.

One night, Jon and I were at a great local bar called The Nelson House. This bar had no televisions and was your true, old-fashioned, blue-collar bar. It was where the farmers would go after plowing the fields, and sometimes bluegrass music would play in the background. It was a mellow place to chill.

Jon and I would spend nights there talking. It was great. This one night in particular, was my favorite. We were talking politics like we often did, and Jon said something that sparked my attention.

He said, "Dude, you Republicans always jump on socialism. Why are you against people getting proper medical care for free? Americans are so selfish."

I quickly responded, "Because someone has to pay for it, and it's called raising taxes."

"Man, do you even know what the purpose of socialism is?" He was upset at this point. He was flailing his arms and making dramatic gestures. Those sorts of things intimidate me. If you're ever in a discussion with me and want to scare me, just start flailing your arms like a madman.

I just stared blankly and took a sip of my drink hoping that would count as an answer.

"Exactly my point," he went on. "Jesus was a socialist. Jesus didn't worry about what was His. Jesus chose to live poor so others could have more. The very idea of Jesus dying on the cross is a form of socialism. Jesus gave all He had so we could have the gift of eternal life for *free*! You're right. Someone has to pay—and He did."

Again, I just stared at him and finished my drink. Jon shook his head in annoyance and then changed the subject to something he was writing.

Now before all the Christian conservatives start setting fire to my book in a fit of riot rage, let me explain. I'm not suggesting a political agenda by any means, and I'm certainly not saying Jesus was a socialist. Jon significantly missed the mark on that; but the conversation was convicting to say the least. I want to live like Jesus, but how many times do I walk by homeless people and ignore the need? Even worse, I don't even pray for them? How often am I more concerned with what is mine instead of my generosity? How often do I cheat the church with my tithes because my heart's not entirely in it?

The point has nothing to do with politics and has absolutely nothing to do with socialism. The point is this: as a Christian, I cannot claim the name of Jesus if I am not going to live with the attributes of Christ. And I certainly cannot choose the attributes I want. Through relationship with Christ, I develop the heart, convictions, and passions of God. Jesus wasn't a socialist, He was just modeling the attributes of His Father.

"Like, totally, no way!"

My wife is fairly predictable. Her behavior is consistent, and she doesn't desire a lot of spontaneity in her life. While I on the other hand, love to be different. I'm always getting into new ideas, adventures, activities, etc. But like most girls, she has her "special button." And no this is not a sexual reference. This special button only gets pushed when a certain friend of hers comes around. And let me just say, I have never been more amused and annoyed at the same time. It's quite the complex.

Now while this chapter was marinating in my brain, I witnessed this special occasion take place, and there it was: another wonderful example of this "mirroring trait." Now this friend of hers is a girly girl. She's blonde, talks like one although she's deceptively smart, and has the superpower to make my lovely wife turn Hulk and transform into this "thing." This thing I did not marry.

I start to see my wife's head bob a bit more, there's a massive incline in the usage of the word "like," and she'll end her sentences with this elongated ditzy slurring as if she is ending her sentences with a terrible French accent.

I've never told her what I notice when she's around this friend, but this time, I decided it was time. "So, every time you're around her, you change."

"Nuh uh. No I don't," she replied. Then seeing me raise my eyebrows and slowly nod my head yes, she continued, "Wait. Really? I do? How?"

"Well, for starters, you talk ditzy; like a blonde. And you use the word 'like' a lot."

Laughing out loud she replied, "Oh my, I can't believe it. I didn't even realize it. It's like when you started using British words when you hung out with Jon."

We have this unrelenting urge to mirror those we love. Friends, family, mentors, it doesn't matter. I started using British lingo because I was hanging out with Jon frequently. I didn't one day decide I liked the word fancy. What happens is we start mirroring attributes of people when we've been exposed to them for a while. It's a subconscious thing. You know what I'm talking about. When you were a kid during summer break, you would spend an entire week at a friends house, and by the end of the week you found yourself laughing like they did or walking like they did. I started using the word fancy because subconsciously, it further connected me with Jon—whether I knew it or not. It works the same way with Christ. If you spend a lot of time with Him, you will start to mirror His attributes and I realized it certainly doesn't always happen quickly and automatically. You may realize it, you may not, but I guarantee others will notice.

The bad business man

I heard a story once about a pastor who mentored a bad man. This man's life was just awful, and he did some terrible things with little regret. Through God's divine intervention, God used this pastor to lead this man to Christ. After his conversion, this man set out to become a Christian entrepreneur and was quite successful. It was a pretty inspiring story—if it had stopped there. But despite his success, he still felt empty inside and began to meet with this pastor about it. What came out of those meetings were the realities of how ungodly his business practices were. In fact, so ungodly, that it would even make some non-Christian people's jaws drop. One day, while meeting, the pastor shed some light into this mans spiritual battle. What the pastor said to this man will stick with me for the rest of my life. The pastor leaned over the table during their meeting and said the following:

"You know what I love about you? You have the heart of Christ. You know what I can't stand about you? You have the character of Satan and you make God sick."

Could you imagine cleaning yourself up after a past lifestyle like his and still be told that? But I think that's just it. I remember surrendering my life to Christ for the first significant time in my life. It was a mess.

I remember being in high school when I surrendered my life to Christ. I was stoked. I was telling everyone about it, reading my Bible religiously, praying constantly, and cursing the secular world. I even threw all my "non-Christian" albums away. I was involved in the youth group band, never partied, rarely used cuss words, and made sure people knew why.

You know those people that work eighty hours a week and make you feel bad about it; as if working a normal work week is being complacent? Or those moms who suddenly think their method of parenthood is the absolute best and the rest is crap? Yeah, I was that guy. "Oh, you listen to *that* band?"

In my mind, I was a good Christian. I was doing all things I thought should be done. I had the heart of Christ. Yet, in the midst of all that, I would go to the gym and purposely pick the elliptical machine directly behind an attractive girl wearing tight yoga pants. Or purposely sneak into an R-rated movie because I knew there was nudity.

I wasn't a bad person. In fact, I had a good heart and great intentions. The problem was my character. The attributes of God weren't a bi-product of a relationship. I immediately skipped the relationship portion and dove into the "product." If I was going to be a Christian, I needed to manifest a visible change.

I think that is what happened to that man. After being so invested into a terrible lifestyle, surrendering his life to Christ didn't automatically change his character. His heart, yes, but not his character.

Lots of snowballs on Mt. Everest

See I have this problem. My wife calls it "snowballing" and you read all about it in the last chapter. But in case you are lazy and didn't read the last chapter or just skimmed the chapter like a jerk, here's a brief synopsis. What I like to do, is take a very minor problem I'm having and snowball it into this massive problem. And it usually ends with us all dying.

I was having one of those snowball days where I sat in my car in rush hour traffic totally imprisoned by my thoughts. I was thinking about my spirituality and relationship with God. As usual, I was making the situation out to be worse than it was.

I was on staff at a church, and yet it had been weeks—probably months—since I spent quality time with God. My prayers were scarce and when they existed at all, they were as shallow as the wives from *The Real Housewives* TV shows. I couldn't get past the fact that I must be a fake. Like a modern day version of a Pharisee from the Bible, except better acted than the modern day rendition of Romeo and Juliet with Leonardo DiCaprio.

The conclusion, as usual, was that I was going to die. But this time, literally and spiritually. After I died from being homeless, my soul wouldn't carry on to heaven but rather spiral down to hell where I would spend eternity burning up and probably smelling roasted marshmallows in perpetuity but never being allowed to eat one.

The battle I was having was between being a "good" Christian and a "bad" Christian. Even though I was in ministry, grew up in the church, surrendered my life to God, rid my life of worldly junk, there were still days, weeks, and months where I felt so far away from God. Then the question hit me, "Should I even be in ministry?"

It was then that I had this realization. Our spirituality is a lot like climbing Mt. Everest. We can't just spontaneously decide to climb Mt. Everest, we'd literally die. In order to climb Mt. Everest, we have to prepare. We have to plan out our preparations, and we have to plan out our climb. The preparation is rigorous and is getting us into a position to simply *attempt* the climb. All the preparation in the world can't even guarantee our success on the climb. It merely gives us the physical endurance and the mental sharpness to deal with the mountain's challenges.

Here's the kicker. Even after all that preparation and planning, we still can't just climb to the top. We'd literally die from the altitude if the other stuff doesn't whack us first. We have to set up a base camp and make sure we have all the gear we need to start. Then we begin climbing in increments. We climb a little, set up camp, adjust to the altitude, communicate back to base camp on our progress, and prepare to climb a little farther the next day.

But the mountain, in all its beauty, has its unpredictable challenges. And sometimes, as we are climbing little by little, we encounter certain challenges that throw us off guard which can force us back down the mountain a bit to regain our traction.

And I'm convinced that as loose as this analogy is, it's a snapshot into our spiritual lives. We are all climbing Mt. Everest, and some of us are farther up the mountain than others. And as any climber will tell you, it's not a race. Climbing takes patience, skill, and being well-equipped for the journey.

————————————

I think to some degree we all have this same battle.
"I don't read my Bible enough,"
"My prayers aren't long enough and eloquently spoken,"
"I'm not convicted on these things like those people are."
"I'm reading the Bible and praying everyday, so why am I still struggling with this sin?"

And because of those things, we can tend to categorize ourselves as "bad" Christians. We can start to poison our minds thinking because we are stumbling in areas of life, we do not have a good relationship with God.

I think all of us who identify ourselves as Christians, would agree that we truly want to live with the attributes of God. I don't think there is anyone questioning that. So with the heart of Christ and pure intentions, we strive to accomplish it. And what we end up doing is trying to climb straight to the top of Mt. Everest.

It's foolish to think that the man that pastor mentored would suddenly know how to run a Christian business after a lifestyle of habitual sin with no repentance. He needed to plan and prepare. He tried to climb Mt. Everest ill-equipped and ended up back at base camp.

I don't think it's about whether my relationship with God is good or bad, I think it's about the journey; the pursuit. God wants worshippers who are after His own heart. I'm gonna have seasons of distractions and challenges. But that's what makes

Mt. Everest . . . Everest. It's the challenges. In the pursuit, the question then becomes, how equipped am I to deal with the challenges? In those challenging seasons, I can identify where I need to be better equipped, and I climb back down a little, address the issues, and keep climbing. This way, the next time the challenge presents itself, I'll be ready.

I didn't meet Jon and suddenly start talking with British lingo. I hung out with him and spent time getting to know him and everything he was about. I debated politics with him and before I knew it, I was talking like him. Living with the attributes of Christ is a process. It's a daily climb. So, I insert disciplines in my life to prepare myself for the climb and its challenges. And that's what God wants from me. He wants me to pursue His heart and, in the process, He'll refine me and make me stronger for the climb.

MURDERING SANTA

There was a period in my life where I thought I was the king of pranks. I thought about making a trophy and hosting a celebration to award myself the prize. It would be a glorious event. Black tie would not be optional, only the best wine would be served, and the event would be emceed by Jimmy Fallon. I am convinced Jimmy Fallon and I would great friends, so I figure this would be the best opportunity to test that theory.

I must not conceal, however, I wasn't twelve-years old when I put my sisters' underwear in the freezer. No. In fact, I was nine-teen years old and put a kid on my dorm floor's underwear in his mini-fridge freezer over a holiday weekend he was gone.

My pranks were not often designed with solid engineering. In fact, they were crafted very carelessly and lacked a certain maturity level. Although, I was quite clever in my approach. If I was going to get caught, why do it alone? Being the persuader

The Ugly Couch

I am, I always managed to pull in a handful of people to execute the pranks with me usually splitting people's irritation among all of us instead of just on me. Some of the consequences to my pranks were minuscule and the consequences didn't outweigh the benefits, most of the time.

One evening, the kid with the frozen underwear came in to our dorm and shouted about how he found five-hundred feet of yellow camping rope in the dumpster. Paul had an affinity for dumpster diving. One time in particular, he came into the dormitory boasting of his findings. He had found a full bottle of wine and a typewriter. He drank the wine that night and proceeded to write the rest of his semesters papers on the typewriter.

I suggested we prank the second floor with the rope. They were our rivals, and we disliked a majority of them. My plan involved using the rope to tie all the doors together. We decided to tie them crisscross across the hallway so when one opened the door it tightened the others. In the peak of the night, we executed our plan. After the rope was all tied up, I wasn't satisfied with our work. I decided we needed something annoying to entice them to the hallway they couldn't access. Paul informed us that he had an air-horn in his desk drawer.

"Of course you do, Paul," I said chuckling to myself. "Go and get it!"

Paul skipped on down to his room and retrieved his air-horn. We decided we would tie the trigger with a rubber band and to toss it down the hallway like a grenade waking them all up at 2:30 in the morning. Of course, I miscalculated the other fifty people in our dormitory and the their ability to call campus police.

On another occasion, I decided I would prank one of the guys from second floor I didn't like. I convinced some guys from my floor to help. The plan was to staple together 1080 paper Dixie cups and put them outside his dorm door. We then proceeded to fill the cups with all kinds of liquids like old milk, Gatorade, ketchup, and more. There was no way he was going to get out of his dorm without stepping on the cups spilling the contents of the cups everywhere. It was a genius plan. Except, I miscalculated once again. I didn't consider that this kid had an exam that next morning and couldn't miss it. So he stepped on the cups crushing milk and ketchup into the carpet. And unlike lightning, I was prone to strike in the same place twice. So the second floor Resident Assistant knew who to hunt down. We were forced to clean up the mess for him and were fined fifty dollars each to cover the damage to the carpet.

Poor Santa

Among the harmless pranks I pulled, such as my friend hiding in a suitcase naked or prank calling the TBN television station, I had some unfortunate experiences where I lacked significant discernment in my pranks. And I know what you're thinking, how is a guy, naked in a suitcase using discernment? Well let me assure you, he wasn't fully naked. He was wearing a sock and it was in an all guys dorm. That makes it okay.

In fact there are two stories in particular in which my pranks had consequences I wasn't comfortable living with.

During the evenings in college, boredom ensued quite regularly. Sometimes, Paul, the kid with the frozen underwear, would show up with a suitcase full of cigars and we would smoke them; other times we would pull pranks. One of our regular, favorite pranks was to drive around the surrounding neighborhoods and swap and/or rearrange lawn decorations. Especially during holiday times, we loved to put that persons blow up turkey in the neighbors yard; stuff like that. And sometimes, we would take items for our dorms. I'm not talking about serious stuff. Usually it would be a lawn gnome that was covered in leaves. They clearly didn't care about it, and it made a great bathroom decoration. I named him Curtis.

One night in particular, around the Christmas season, we decided to make it into a game. We loaded up into three cars, set a time to return and said whoever came back with the biggest and best lawn gear, would win. After an hour or so of racing around, trying to fit plastic reindeer in our cars, we all reunited at our spot and evaluated the collections. And after determining a winner, we set back out to put the items back; in their neighbors yards of course. In that moment, I had a brilliant idea for me and my roommate. He is actually now my brother-in law.

I remember when he first saw a picture of my little sister. He took a look at her cheerleading picture and said, "Dude, your sister . . ." to which I replied, "Dude, she's fifteen." He then responding as if he had thought of alternative solutions said, "Dude, when she's eighteen . . . " Of course when she was eighteen or nineteen, he asked her out and she said no. I laughed at him. Then one day, after we were roommates, I logged onto Facebook and saws picture of them kissing. I freaked out, called him, and pretended to be upset that he didn't ask my permission first. In all reality, I thought it was awesome at the potential of my best friend actually becoming my brother.

Well, I convinced my roommate that we should keep one of the items for our dorm. Calvin chose the biggest inflatable Santa that lit up with lights and had mechanical arms and a head. We took it back, set it up, and began boasting of our newest dorm member. One of the guys on our floor thought it was a bad thing to do and began to scold us. He cussed us out and told us if we didn't return the stolen, very expensive Santa, he was going to turn us in to the police. Afraid of the police, we packed up Santa and attempted to return it. Only problem was, we didn't remember what house Santa belonged to. Faced with the dilemma, we chose the option only a nineteen-year-old college student would choose; we killed Santa. We threw him in the river. When we returned to campus, we informed the student we had safely returned Santa to his rightful owner. Plagued with guilt that we had broken the law, I never played that prank again.

"He likes you, he likes you not"

The second story involves the killing of zero Santa's, but does have zero redeeming qualities to it.

It was around the era when Facebook was just becoming popular and people were unaware of the effects this public forum could have on one's life. Without caution, people uploaded all of their personal information in the hopes that we could look up people from our universities. Without the awareness of the privacy holes, college girls would post their cell phone numbers blindly to this site. Well, of course I was going to come up with a prank for that.

Through the art of Facebook stalking and a source from

our dorm building, it became very clear that one particular gal was quite fond of this guy from one of her classes and it just so happened that we didn't like him that much. What wasn't clear, however, was whether the feelings were mutual between him and her. They had been communicating, but it appeared she liked him more than he liked her, and we thought it would be a great opportunity to make him look bad.

We decided to call her pretending to be him. She was quite excited when we told her who was calling. She totally bought it. The fact she was dumb enough to believe we were calling from "his grandmothers phone" and our voice sounded weird because "he was sick," allowed me to justify the prank in my mind that she deserved it for being stupid anyway.

Pretending to be this guy, we asked her on a date. She was giddy. We set up the whole date and assured her the feelings she had toward us were mutual. The prank seemed hilarious in my head. The plan was this: She would show up at the restaurant, all dressed up, and he would never show up. I had hilarious visions of her screaming and yelling at him for standing her up, while he stood there confused at what she was saying.

The date was set. They would meet Sunday evening for dinner and a movie. Sunday night came and went and of course this guy never showed up for his date and she was very upset.

Unbeknownst to me, this guy and gal quickly assessed this was a prank and they quickly found out who the source was. She was no longer upset at this kid, but upset with us instead; then things got worse.

We heard shouting and doors slamming one afternoon in our dorm shortly after the prank. This guy came storming into our dormitory completely fuming with anger and had the student who had actually made the call up against the wall and fists were about to fly. This situation got out of hand real fast and now blood was about to be shed.

A few others and I quickly flooded the scene and stopped the fight before there was blood, but not before this poor girls heart got broken, and not before we prematurely revealed to this girl that he did in fact, actually like her but was planning a formal courtship.

A beautiful terrain

Pranks can be fun, but they can be equally destructive without a moral compass. I've often reflected on my pranks to the contrast of living my life in faith and Scripture.

I've spent most of my life as a Christian. And when you have a Christian upbringing like mine, you can easily compromise boundaries. Spending most of my life as the "good kid" clouded my spiritual judgment because I always thought, *At least I'm not getting hammered in a fraternity and having a bunch of sex with girls.*

But that's where the lessons of these pranks came into play in my own life. I had stopped reading Scripture regularly, and I stopped living with a spiritual compass. I merely categorized myself as a "good kid" because I wasn't practicing what the Christian society classified as "bad."

We need to be careful of the boundaries we live by. We can easily draw hard lines in the sand and mark them as good but take one more step and it's suddenly bad. Jesus didn't live His life that way and neither should we. Jesus lived His life with a

73

spiritual compass. He lived a life in constant relationship with His Father and the rest flowed from that.

What if we focused on loving like Jesus and studying Scripture to learn more about our Savior? If we focus on being walking results of God's grace and sovereignty, soon our spiritual lives will point to true north.

Pranks are pranks. But there's a difference between putting someone's underwear in the freezer and murdering an inflatable Santa. Putting someone's underwear in the freezer isn't the really that bad, but it's still not something I would put on a resume. Killing Santa, however, does make a statement on my character and about how quickly my pranks progressed into destructive behavior that involved stealing, vandalism, and lying.

And just like pranks, Christians are Christians. None are perfect, and Jesus doesn't expect us to be. But there's a difference between living a life shaped by God's grace and Scripture and living a life just occupying a seat in church on Sunday mornings. What's wrong with occupying a seat on Sunday mornings? Nothing. Except that you're just being wasted talent for the Kingdom. When you embrace God's grace and advance into the Kingdom, you have a lot to offer, and God wants to use you. You're like a beautiful terrain.

But when you just sit there, not growing spiritually, not watering the terrain with spiritual rain, you find other ways to keep your faith alive. You think that the more you attend church the better you are, if you raise your hands in worship you are magically more spiritual, or if you go to that couples' class, then you're finally doing what you need to do to be good in God's eyes. But guess what? God doesn't have eyes. Well, okay, maybe He does. I guess I don't really know. But that's not the point. I do know that I encounter God every time I have hot wings because, well, hot wings will be in heaven.

You don't have to prove anything to God. You're not staying spiritually watered to be good. You water your faith, because when you water a beautiful terrain it stays beautiful and flourishes. People begin to recognize its beauty and want to be a part of it. We need to have a faith that flourishes so much and is so beautiful people see God through you.

Since Christians aren't perfect, our terrain isn't going to be perfect. We will find weeds, have dry spouts, and more. So, we have to stay on top of our faith by staying in Scripture and growing spiritually. Otherwise our spiritual lives will slowly decline until the lines are so blurred that we diminish Christianity to good and bad, and we will mistake weeds for flowers and bushes. Oh, and you will also murder an inflatable Santa.

THE HOT MUGSHOT GUY

I love beer. In fact, I love all alcohol. Yes; I said it. I'm a pastor and I like a cold, delicious pint of beer. I like Pinot Grigio, martinis, and sipping the occasional Scotch. Being a pastor and liking alcohol seem to go together like being a Christian and being a Democrat. People just think they cannot co-exist. I believe this is the case because a lot of Christians cannot separate the perception of consuming alcohol and being drunk. It's almost as if the majority of Christians assume if you drink alcohol at all, you can only do so by putting your poison of choice in a plastic red cup, blasting dirty rap music, and slurping Jell-O shots off the belly buttons of sorority girls.

A short while back, I was helping a guy move with a bunch of other Christians and one NASCAR fan—he was wearing a Jeff Gordon shirt. This NASCAR fan was a friend of the guy moving, but not a friend of the other Christians. Not knowing Christians would be there, this guy brought a six-pack of beer to the moving party as a generous gift. The Christians pretended to be nice to this guy because he was drinking beer.

After the move was wrapping up, the NASCAR fan had to leave. After saying his goodbyes to everyone he headed toward the door. As he approached the door, he turned around and with a joyful spirit said, "Have good day everyone! Enjoy the beer! I'll leave it here for you all to enjoy!" He smiled, feeling good about his generosity. Now in normal human fashion, any normal person, even if you weren't a beer drinker, would respond with something like this: "Thanks man! Appreciate the gift! Have a good day, too!" And then just not drink it. However, in response to this man's generous gift, one of the Christians responded with an arrogant flare, a condemning tone and with his arms crossed he said, "Oh, well, I don't drink alcohol." With defeat written all over his face, the NASCAR fan hung his head in embarrassment and left.

Now I'm no theologian, but I would suggest Jesus wouldn't be impressed with the "moral stance" this Christian held so firmly to that day. I think Jesus would have embraced this man, loved on him genuinely, and certainly would not have looked poorly at the man because he brought beer to the party. He might have suggested that it was a sin to bring something pretending to be beer like Miller Lite, and that next time he should bring real beer, not pee water. But again, I'm no theologian.

"If you watch that show, you'll go to hell"

There's a comedy television show I like a lot, but it's a controversial one: *Modern Family*. I'm assuming at this point, the religious people reading this book are getting ready to close this book because I drink alcohol and watch this show. Let me assure you, I have a point, so stick with me.

Modern Family is a comedy television series about a family different from the "norm." It starts with the grandfather, Jay, who is very uptight, conservative, wealthy, and not very attractive, yet he just married a super hot, seductive woman from Columbia, Gloria, that has a son, Manny, in middle school. Everyone assumes the obvious, even the rest of the family at first; Gloria must be a gold digger. Jay has two children, one son, Mitch, and one daughter, Claire, who are grown up with their own families. Claire is married to a goof ball of a character, Phil, and they have three children. Of course, their oldest daughter, Haley, is super promiscuous and Phil and Claire try to contain it, yet often, they do things in everyday life that prove they are still teenagers at heart. Claire, who is also very attractive, struggles with jealousy of this new hot lady Gloria, who is technically her mom now. Then there's Jay's son. He's gay, lives with his partner, Cam, and they adopted a little girl, Lily, from Vietnam. Jay has a really hard time accepting Mitch and his lifestyle, and that tension is stressed throughout the show.

This show is incredibly funny, incredibly acted, incredibly written, and amazingly filmed. So much so that while on the air, it has won multiple Emmy awards and has been nominated countless times. But the controversy is in the fact that Mitch is gay, living a normal home life with his partner, adopted a girl, and the rest of the family live far from Christian lifestyles. And as Christians, watching this show is a *big* deal.

I've heard more conversations than I would like to have

heard about how terrible the show is and how it's the reason our society is corrupt. And I've had way too many conversations with people who condemn me for watching the show myself and actually liking it. I'm sure there are people reading right now who condemn me for watching it. The truth is, I love the show. I think the show reflects life situations incredibly well and is incredibly funny.

At the end of season five of the show, Mitch and Cam actually got married. It was a huge part of the show that they even split it into two episodes. With those last two episodes revolving around this wedding, all the things that could go wrong, did. All the details started to fall a part, to the extent that they almost were not be able to have their wedding. At the same time, Jay was having an extremely difficult time accepting his son was marrying another man. He was struggling with the pride as a man that his son was gay. Jay was embarrassed by this situation and didn't really contribute much to the wedding. Mitch began to feel upset because he knew that if the tables were turned and the situation was happening to his sister, Jay would have called in the Calvary, told all his friends, showcased the wedding at his country club, and boastfully expressed his excitement.

However, because Mitch was gay and Jay had an issue with it, he wasn't proud of his son and he didn't hide how he felt about it. This made Mitch upset. But toward the end of the two part episode, Jay came to his senses and realized his role as a father. To unconditionally love his son, support him, and be proud of him—despite how he felt. The dad pulled some strings, and they ended up having the wedding at his country club. He even walked his son down the isle and did it with pride.

The issue people have with this show is people believe if Christians watch this show, then they are condoning the lifestyle they live in the show. Most people I've heard or had conversations with would air on the politically-correct side and state that they don't like the show because of its "morals." But when challenged, it becomes increasingly clear it's really because of the gay couple and how the show just promotes them living a "normal" lifestyle.

Well guess what? They do live a fairly normal lifestyle besides the fact that they are wealthy. And the shows morals? If you would watch it, you would see how strong family morals are actually presented. The show's life blood pumps around the family unit and how important support, love, and relationships are within the family. It shows how important it is to raise your kids up right and to be kind, loving people. And how even though the family screws up all the time, there is reconciliation and unconditional love towards each other.

Listen, maybe I shouldn't watch it. I don't know. There's no verses in Scripture that tells me what shows to watch. But there is a Holy Spirit to give each of us personal convictions. It's not a noble act to condemn a show that actually promotes a healthy family unit in terms of non-Christian morals simply because a couple is gay. Do I think the gay lifestyle reflects the truths of Scripture? Absolutely not. Do I believe in what Scripture promotes as an acceptable marriage union? You bet I do. But watching that show doesn't mean I like gay couples getting married.

The problem here is that Christians condemn and judge like this when non-Christian people don't live their lives according to Scripture. But if they don't claim to be Christians, we can't hold them to that kind of accountability. That's like working for a company that makes you wear formal clothes everyday and during a business meeting with a client, in your head you begin condemning them for wearing jeans, simply because it's tacky and unprofessional. They don't even work for the same company with those guidelines.

Society doesn't live by Scripture because they don't believe in it, so we cannot hold them accountable to it. It's that simple. What you can do is love on them like the Jesus from our Scriptures so much they are confused by the over-abundance of generosity, humility, kindness, and love we show to others. We can pray for them. We can pray they will encounter God. We can be their friends without the agenda to "save them." But when the opportunity comes to share that gift with them and hope they accept it, we should share it. And what if they don't accept it? We continue to love them anyway. It's after they meet Jesus the reconciliation in their lifestyles can begin.

God knows the condition of my heart. He knows when I watch *Modern Family* I'm not condoning the lifestyle. However, shows that flaunt, promote and perversely show nudity, or close to it, I cannot watch. Not because I'm a Christian, but because I'm a sinful person who struggles with lust like every man in the world. I cannot watch those shows because of the way they tempt my spirit. I have a very high personal conviction on this. What I'm not saying is that you should go watch porn, "Just because I'm watching it doesn't mean I agree with it." That's just stupid.

Somehow we can fall to the notion that God's *unconditional* love is not applicable to gays and non-Christians yet it does apply to me even though I struggle with lust all the time. Really? How many Christian men have pornography addictions but will hold a moral stance against a show like *Modern Family* because of a gay couple. It's similar to people who condemn drinking alcohol, which Jesus consumed Himself in Scripture, yet fill their bodies daily with the absolutely worst form of gluttony possible. Think about how many Christians hate on alcohol yet drink gallons of soda and eat fast food nearly every day. I know Christians who condemn alcohol consumption, but they have to have a can of Pepsi everyday; which is probably worse than beer. Or condemn gay marriage but stuff their faces with ungodly amounts of food and never exercise. How many Christians are obese and don't take care of the body God gave them? How many Christians hate on gay couples but are absolutely slaves to their financial debts because they are not good stewards of the money God entrusted them with? The answer is that all of us are completely and utterly flawed and worth condemnation, but God's love is so unconditional it covers us all.

The hot mug shot guy

A photo went viral not too long ago, cycling Facebook and Twitter so fast that it became a phenomenon. It was the mug shot of a guy who got arrested for gang-related activity. Why was his photo circulating? Because he was hot. Seriously. This criminal was so attractive even his mug shot had girls drooling over their keyboards despite the fact he was a felon. This photo became so popular a Los Angeles modeling agency scooped him up and gave him a modeling contract.

The Ugly Couch

Let me explain this some more. This guy is a convicted felon. He even served two years in jail for grand theft. This time, he was a arrested for a serious weapons charge. Yep, a convicted criminal with a serious rap sheet gets a modeling contract that will pay him ridiculous amounts of money despite his knack for getting arrested for stupidity.

How does a convicted criminal advance in this world for doing something wrong? Doesn't seem fair.

Here's what I love about this story. As twisted and just downright crazy as it sounds, this nonsense reminds me of our relationships with God. Because that's what God's grace sounds like to most people; crazy nonsense. As dumb and stupid as the human race is, it just seems like nonsense that God would love us the way Scripture tells us He does.

We are just like Hot Mug Shot Guy. We all do stupid things and insist on doing them over and over and over again. Some of our stupidity comes with more serious consequences comparative to Hot Mug Shot Guy's two years in jail. Yet while we may be sitting in jail, feeling the bondage of our failures, there's a God out there, like this modeling agency, who looks at our mug shot and sees our beauty, not our rap sheet. Then on top of that, offers us a deal that seems just ridiculous. God offers us the ultimate payment: His grace. It's a salary we don't deserve, and it makes no sense that we would be offered it when God knows we're just gonna continue to screw up. All we have to do is accept it and begin reconciliation. Begin the new life, because our God is a God of second chances. Third chances. Fourth chances. Infinity chances.

A living testimony

All my life there has been one word and even a phrase that has been a part of my Christian lingo and a part of the Christian culture. It's the word "testimony." Now the word testimony literally means "evidence provided by the appearance of something." So in the Christian world, this is supposed to represent the evidence of your faith provided by the appearance of God's grace in your life.

Over time, however, this phrase came to life: "hurting your testimony." While a noble concept, that we don't want to do things that are evidence of an ungodly life, it has morphed into quite the large list of dos and don'ts. Initially, it started out as the concept if you were in a bar, getting hammered, and getting into bar fights, it's probably not a good idea because doing that would start to creep into your life and people would start to associate your faith with the evidence of you getting drunk; which is a sin. Again a noble and truthful concept.

What it has become is a standard phrase used to fuel religion. And the meaning behind testimony has been reduced down to a list of moral things you have done and the things you don't do because you're not a bad person. In essence it has reduced the work the Holy Spirit has done in your life to the fact you are now too righteous to watch a television show. And in finality, the Christian walk has been reduced to solely avoid things that will hurt your testimony. 2 Sam. 12:14 NASB

The reality is this: you cannot hurt your testimony. You can't hurt it, because you're not responsible for it and you're selfish if you think you are. Our testimony is this: *we are terrible people and God's grace is sufficient for all our failures.* Our testimony is

2 Corinthians 12:9: "But He said to me, 'My grace is sufficient for you, for my power is made perfect in weakness.' Therefore I will boast all the more gladly of my weaknesses, so that the power of Christ may rest upon me."

Our weaknesses and failures are what gives us a testimony. Paul is proud of the fact he is weak so God's power can redeem him. God doesn't care about your rap sheet. We all have a rap sheet. So we need to stop trying to have a perfect rap sheet, listen to our convictions, and just love like Jesus. Because I can take a moral stance against a show with a gay couple in it because my biblical convictions don't support that kind of marriage, but it doesn't change the fact that I still struggle with lust daily, and have a gluttony problem. It doesn't change the fact that, when I open a bag of Doritos, I have to fight the urge to be gluttonous and eat the entire bag. It doesn't change the fact I have anger issues. It doesn't change the fact I'm a bad person and still need God's grace to cover me and make me strong in His strength.

This is where God's gift of the Holy Spirit comes into play. Not everyone struggles with gluttony. But I do. So the Holy Spirit sends me high convictions about that kind of stuff. When you are Christian, the Holy Spirit lovingly sends these convictions into our hearts. They are caution signs of the things we struggle with. I know a lot of people who have had a bad experience with alcohol. Maybe a parent abused the substance, or maybe they struggled with it themselves. The Holy Spirit sends them high convictions on the issue, and they cannot have a sip of it or even be around it because of the temptation to abuse again or simply just the wisdom to not be around it to avoid possibility of it resurfacing.

Me on the other hand, I don't have those high convictions toward alcohol, because it's never been a temptation in my life. I can have beer and not be tempted to indulge in drunkenness. But I do struggle with lust. So I can not watch shows with nudity, skimpy dressing, and other things of the sort because of the temptations it provides me. I know some people who have high convictions about technology and social media because of the effect it has on their real lives. So they either limit their use or don't use it at all. Does that mean that the Internet should be banned? Of course not.

I am a pastor who likes alcohol. Therefore, I drink it in a fashion that is honorable to the people I pastor. I know being a pastor, I'm going to encounter people who drink all the time and people who can't drink at all because of a high conviction with it. So as per my own personal conviction as a pastor, I choose very carefully where or when I drink alcohol in public, in the town I pastor. Because I know people in my ministry who struggle with it. Other than that, I don't apologize for drinking it.

We don't live our lives to "help" or "hurt" our testimony. That's religion. We need to live our lives in the hope and redemption through God's power in our weakness. Because we are all sinful people. We are all sinners with different convictions and temptations.

This doesn't excuse us to be disobedient to Scripture. I think that's obvious. This isn't a license to jump into a sinful lifestyle and think it's okay because "God loves me regardless." That is true, but Scripture is clear on what happens when you receive God's grace and blatantly live in sin without repentance and redemption. Your faith has to present evidence of God's Spirit, otherwise you're just a lair.

God calls us to act in justice, love, mercy, and kindness, and to walk humbly with Him—not to boast in our religious condemnations. I'm not saying to crack open the vodka at Bible studies, because that's just stupid. What I am saying is we need to think less of ourselves and realize that our testimonies rely on the fact we have a rap sheet and will continue to add to it whether we like it our not. We just have to learn to accept the fact that we "Christians" are not above the gay couple on television getting married.

THE STARBUCKS
OF ISRAEL

It's hard being me. I think a lot of it has to do with how awesome I am. I try to contain it, but when you deal with the mediocre people I do on a daily basis, it's hard for the awesomeness to not creep in. Wherever I go, people want to talk to me, girls want to hang out with me, and kids want to be like me. I'm not saying all of this with a false humility either. It's just a fact. I'm super fit, and good looking in a Brad Pitt kind of way. I'm friends with "The Situation" from the *Jersey Shore* and we "GTL" (gym, tanning, laundry) every day.

When I go to Starbucks, the baristas all know my name. In case you're not awesome like me and don't know what a barista is, it's an awesome name for the chump making my coffee. I make sure I say my order in a complex way and say it really fast. This ensures I'm a regular customer to all the people with headphones, who are pretending to listen to music but actually eavesdropping on everyone else in a judgmental way. This also proves to them I'm wealthy enough to buy Starbucks every day. I order a quad venti, skinny vanilla latte with two parts soy milk and three parts skim milk, extra hot, add caramel—and lots of it, two Splenda, one Equal, four raw sugars, no foam (there better be no stupid foam), light whipped cream, a few ice cubes, double cupped and topped with chocolate sprinkles.

I wear sunglasses inside and play on my iPhone the whole time so those around me see I have an iPhone. Plus it also looks like I'm answering very important emails. Then when I get my drink, I make sure to take a photo and share it on the fourteen social media sites where I'm a member.

I think the hardest thing about being awesome all the time is being a dad. My daughter just doesn't seem to understand the significance I hold and insists on trying to steal my awesomeness. She commands all the attention, makes us change her diapers, and even makes us feed her for goodness sake.

Now if you know me at all, you know how untrue all of that is. If you don't know me, let me fill you in. I'm chubby, I don't know the *Jersey Shore* cast and, like most of America, I binge watch the show on Netflix. When I go to Starbucks, which isn't as often as one might think, it's usually with a gift card others purchased for me. Now, maybe the iPhone thing is true, but I think we are all guilty of that one. The people I deal with on a daily basis are way more awesome and talented than me, and my daughter is so awesome she was born saved. My wife is incredible, and she's way cooler than me.

Welcome to Starbucks

There was a point in my life where I actually worked at Starbucks as a transitional job, and my time there was fantastic. However, we occasionally had some customers who must have mistaken their identities with the bratty girl from the Willy Wonka story.

I was running the cash register, shortly after Christmas, when I had an interesting encounter with a customer. After ordering her ridiculous six-dollar drink, she handed me a gift card to purchase it with. I swiped the card and after finishing the transaction, I handed back her card with a receipt and said, "You have four dollars remaining on your card. Thanks!" She took the card and receipt, looked at whoever was with her and snidely commented, "Only a $10 gift card!? Are you kidding me!? Wow!" She then named the people who gifted her the card and labeled them "cheap skates," but used a very different adjective. "Maybe next year they'll only get a $10 gift card from me."

While you may be thinking that this gal was probably fifteen years old max, the sad fact is she was at least thirty. In that moment, her heart of entitlement was exposed. This gal truly thought she was so awesome a $10 gift card was beneath her. I don't know about you, but I get excited when I get two cents off a gallon of gas.

Entitlement

This heart of entitlement doesn't just fall specifically on the type of people I described in the beginning of the chapter. This is an epidemic that we all struggle with: *our own entitlement issues*. And usually, they are worse than we realize. We may think we are so much less entitled and selfish than others, but when we dig deep, we realize we all struggle with feelings of entitlement regardless of how big or small. Let's examine this a bit more.

Maybe we are devoted followers of Christ. We read our Bibles every day and even take notes. Of course we don't have private notes. We don't want to deprive anyone of our awesome revelations, so we make sure we post them on Facebook. This way when the pastor gives a convicting sermon on evangelism and sharing the gospel with others, we aren't convicted. We pray before dinner, and while it's the same boring prayer every night, at least we are praying. We go to church every Sunday, and when the church posts the sermon videos or podcasts on the Internet, we make sure to "share" them on social media and email them to everyone we know. We only listen to Christian radio, and on Sundays, we even sing the songs out loud. We don't watch movies and TV shows that talk about sex or even give a hint of pre-marital encounters. We don't really drink any alcohol, and in our conversations about alcohol we typically say, "Yea, I don't really drink, but I have an occasional glass of wine." Since they drank wine in the Bible, it's okay for us to casually mention it as long we drink in private and not in public. We even take principled oppositions against companies that promote the "liberal" agenda, and we make sure everyone knows that we don't hate people who are gay, but rather hate their sin. And finally, we pay for everything in cash because Dave Ramsey said to. He is the Oprah of the Christian world after all and it would be foolish not to listen to him.

So we live this great "Christian life" and we are convinced we are following God's will for our life and family, and yet things aren't happening the way we think they should be. Our kid's braces are going to cost double what we can actually afford, our kids don't seem to love Jesus as much as we wanted them to, our spouse doesn't love devotional times the way we think he/she should, our debt is catching up to us, and we can't seem to get everyone together for a family night without an argument. This is a heart of entitlement. Because we live a certain way, we subconsciously believe that things should be going differently for us. The reality is, your tire is going to go flat because you ran over a nail. Your tire doesn't care if you read your Bible or not that day.

Maybe we have worked hard for years at our careers and got passed up on a promotion we clearly deserved. We were there twice as long as the person who got it, worked twice as hard, never toyed with the ethical line, and yet we got overlooked. We felt like we deserved it and believe it was unfair.

Maybe entitlement doesn't consume us on that large of a scale, but maybe more of a smaller scale. Maybe we are in line at a fast food joint, and we find ourselves sighing heavily and rolling our eyes because the car in front us is taking forever to order. We have too many places to go and people to see to have to deal with indecisive people like them. Or maybe we refresh our Facebook news feeds and it takes thirty seconds to load. We think it's just ridiculous it takes that long. We need it to load fast because we need to check up on our old classmates to see how much weight they've gained.

Maybe we're at church on Sunday morning and we find ourselves completely annoyed because the service went thirty minutes longer than it normally does. Doesn't the pastor have any regard for people's schedules? We don't mind worshipping Jesus, in fact we find it therapeutic to learn something about the Bible we didn't already know, but keep it to an hour, hour-fifteen max. And the church needs to do a better job at making the services less boring.

That's the problem with entitlement. It creeps into our hearts and sometimes we don't even see it coming. What starts out as an annoyance about the Internet being slow turns into an entitlement that church is all about entertaining us, seeing our friends, learning something new, and not being bored. It eliminates the true purpose of church: *to gather as one unified body to praise and glorify God in our acts of worship.*

———————————

The real issue with entitlement lies deep in our hearts on a more serious foundation. It's the issue of contentment. Life runs at a high speed and it's a challenge to keep up. As I watch the world pass me by, I squint my eyes to see what everyone is running after and before you know it, I'm running with them. So, what is it exactly everyone is running after? Instant gratification.

We are all chasing different things, but the motives are the same. For most of us, the pursuit of money is consuming.

Whether we are chasing that six-figure salary or we are con-stantly chasing money just to get ahead of expenses, we are consumed with it. We want that nice or new house, the nice neighborhood, the new car, the newest gadgets, the biggest TV, the cleanest house, the most well-behaved family, the cool-est church, the best sports team, the perfect job and if your iPhone is a year and a half old, you certainly deserve a new one. Regardless of what we are chasing, we are constantly on the carousel of discontentment. We feel discontent because we feel we deserve better.

Growing up, our family Christmas traditions were always important to me. When I was younger, I would feel ashamed at the fact I only got a fourth as many presents as my friends, but as I got older, those feelings of shame didn't seem to mat-ter as much. My gift lists got shorter, and I wasn't focused on what I wanted and what I didn't get. I remember one specific Christmas when I asked for a new game system. I was so excited because I had a feeling that was the year I was going to get it. On Christmas morning, I proceeded to watch my sisters open this giant Barbie mansion with all these toys. I looked down at my pile with one gift left. I ripped open that gift and what was in it was not a game system. I honestly don't remember what the gift was because I was so distraught about not getting the game system. I smiled, pretended I was thrilled for the gift, and began to feel this massive cloud of entitlement. I really felt like I deserved that game system. Nowadays that I'm married with my own family and a tight budget, we only exchange one or two gifts a year and it doesn't bother me at all. I'm just excited to have my morning fire, read my Christmas story, and have my flavored coffee. On my last Christmas Eve with my mother and sisters, before I moved away to Phoenix, I went to bed sad. I reflected on all the traditions and family fun we had. What I remembered about those Christmases had nothing to do with the gifts, and everything to do with the company. I knew we probably wouldn't get the chance to have Christmas as a family ever again. We would grow up, move away, get married, have kids, etc. The next morning, I woke up to the sound of Christmas music, walked downstairs, and I embraced our traditions one last time. Waking up to the smell of cinnamon buns, egg soufflé, Christmas music playing in the background, snicker-doodle coffee being brewed, and reading a Christmas story together was the best gift I could have ever gotten on that Christmas. It didn't occur to me at the time, but I was content. My mother had no money, and we didn't really exchange many gifts. I was content with no gifts because I didn't feel entitled to any.

Sometimes, the moments we feel most content are the times you realize those moments are going away forever. The lesson I learned growing up was, "Thank God for what you have, trust God for what you need." And in that moment, on that last Christmas morning in our pajamas, I thanked God for my family.

Israel's blessings

The Christian word that often comes to our minds when we talk about entitlement and contentment is the word blessing. We think about that word because we are taught so much about it in the Scriptures. In the King James Version of the Bible, all references to "blessings" appear a total of 522 times. That's a lot of references to God's favor. The Bible talks so much about blessings that we can take it out of context in our own lives.

We often relate blessings with our actions, as if God is sitting on a big fluffy cloud in the sky watching our every move. If we do certain things or say certain things, He will bless us more than the guy next door who drinks Budweiser. We can begin to live our lives in a way where blessings are merely the good consequences of our words or deeds.

Blessings in our lives can sometimes resemble Israel. In 2100 b.c., God comes to Abraham and promises him many descendants and says he is to be the father of a great nation, Israel. Abraham believed in the one true God, which was unlike the people of that day. Then about seven hundred years later, the Israelites are enslaved in Egypt, until Moses comes to their rescue four hundred years later.

Moses leads them out, and they end up wandering the desert for forty years. That is until they finally arrive at the border of the land God promised Abraham. From there, led by the hands of Joshua, they begin to reestablish themselves as Israel by conquering the Promised Land.

While enjoying their sovereignty, they are in full alignment with God. Their nation is not ruled by kings, because they view God as King. Things in Israel are fine and dandy, and then in typical human behavior, the people of Israel start to become discontent. After about three hundred and fifty years, the people of Israel start to feel entitled to a king. They become so entitled that they begin demanding a king. To which God responds in the best parent tone ever, "Fine, I'll give you a king, but you're going to hate it" (a paraphrase of 1 Samuel 8:6-18). Then the Israelites ignore God's words, and in a whiney, pubescent teenager kind of way, they say, "No! We want a king over us. Then we will be like all the other nations, with a king to lead us and to go out before us and fight our battles" (1 Samuel 8:19-20).

So God shrugs His shoulders, and while mumbling to Himself, "You're going to regret this," He gives them what they have been demanding.

Israel goes through a period of roughly one hundred-twenty years where they cycle through three kings: Saul, David, and Solomon. Saul and Solomon turned their backs on God and worshipped the world.

Then as you could predict the progression of the story, Israel splits into two nations, the northern and southern parts. The northern part remained Israel and the southern part which contained Solomon's temple became Judah, and they went to war with each other—often.

After a few hundred years, the Assyrians took over Northern Israel and the Babylonians take over Judah. Then after a couple hundred more years, the Persian king, Cyrus, defeated Babylon and frees the Jews. From there they begin to rebuild the temple and reestablish themselves.

Sometimes our lives and blessings can resemble the story of Israel. We recognize God as the one true God, and He smiles favor on us. He tells us He loves us and will bless us. We are happy in that truth and have peace in Him. Then out of nowhere our lives take a turn for the worse. We become enslaved in Egypt. A family member gets struck down with a terminal illness, our teenage daughter gets pregnant, we lose our jobs and have to foreclose on our house, one of our parents abandons us, and the list goes on. We can speculate why these things happen to us. Maybe it was divine intervention, maybe consequences of prior sins, or maybe wrong place wrong time sort of thing. Before we know it, we are enslaved in our circumstances. We can't seem to break free. What was simply a part of our lives actually become our lives.

Then, miraculously, we are freed. The way it happens varies, but by the grace of God, we pull through. I know for me, God always seems to pull me through a major trial at the last minute. Then we escape the chains of the burdens and trials in our lives only to find ourselves lost. We have been gone so long that we can't seem to find our way back. And after a long, grueling search we find it. Eureka! We fight our way back to our old lives until we get it and begin to rebuild.

Once we get our lives and faith back, it seems like smooth sailing. Our problems have been or are currently being dealt with, and our faith is even stronger in Christ because of it. We start to feel really good because things are going so well that we start to neglect the pressure the outside world is having on our lives. Suddenly we start to become discontent with the little things until it grows and grows. We start to become entitled. God loves us, promised us He would bless us, we suffered some hard trials and came out victorious with an even stronger faith. Therefore, we start looking for that blessing. We start feeling discontent with the life we worked so hard to get back that we begin to feel entitled to a better life than what we have.

It's in those moments where we take our eyes off of God, our one true King and start to look outside the windows at our neighbors. *OCD – NUMBERS – COVETING / MELONS / LEEKS*

"Well they have two cars, why can't we?"

"Their house is bigger than ours and has stainless steel appliances. We want that."

"But everyone who is credible and known wears that style of clothes. We want to look like them."

"Their kid is great in sports; we want our kid to be good too."

"We see their family pictures on Facebook all the time. They seem to be the perfect family. Their pictures are always so perfect."

"How did she get that body after three kids!? I want her post-baby body!"

"They just got the new iPad!? How did they afford that? We wish we could afford stuff like that."

We begin to shift our focus off of Scripture and onto the world causing entitlement. That's when we start demanding things. Meanwhile God is shaking his head saying, "I'll give it to you, but you'll hate it." And of course, we ignore Him and demand it further. And somewhere in the course of all of this, our lives split into two nations: the nation of our desires and the nation of our faith. And they are constantly at war until they both fall, and we find ourselves conquered once again by our sins, and the temple we worked so hard to preserve is leveled.

Our lives and blessings resemble Israel all too well. Like Israel, sometimes God wants to break us in order to bless us. The blessings are often right in front of us and we are too busy looking out the window at the neighbors. And even sometimes the breaking is the blessing.

God doesn't want us to think we are awesome and deserve all this stuff. He wants us to recognize the power we have with Christ in us, and He wants us to adore Him for it. There are so many things to enjoy in this world, and He wants us to enjoy them, but often times we stop enjoying them and start demanding them.

When I struggle with entitlement and discontentment, I just remember Jesus: *a guy who truly was entitled to be worshiped by everyone.* Yet He walked this earth with humility and even helped those who rejected Him. Despite the entitlement He deserved, what did He get? He was hung on a cross with nails driven through his hands and feet. And He did it for us, not Himself.

God wants us to be humbled by a $10 gift card to Starbucks, to be patient when waiting in lines, to spend more time meditating on Scripture than on Facebook, to be totally honored to gather as a local church to glorify Him instead of thinking how the church isn't serving our needs. God wants us to work our jobs in a way that reflects the attributes of Him, and to pursue a genuine relationship with Him that focuses less on our Christian appearances and more on chasing God's heart like David did in the Bible. And most importantly, He wants us to stop seeking instant gratification and discontentment and embrace the eternal satisfaction and true contentment in Him.

CONFESSIONS OF A

FAMILY MAN

"@)@_##&^*@)@0," is essentially what I shouted from the living room of our new Phoenix home. Fatigue had set in as I attempted to hang up floating shelves and curtain hooks in our new living room. I can't quite remember the events exactly, but I know for sure I didn't shout a string of symbols. I shouted some words and phrases I can't put into this book, otherwise it would disqualify me from classifying this book as a "Christian" book. Also, my mom would make me put soap in my mouth and she uses Dial. I prefer Dove.

As you will gather from reading this book, I have Obsessive Compulsive Disorder (OCD), and I like to have things a certain way. Well, when you move to a new home, that's not exactly what you get to experience. Our house was filled with unpacked boxes, empty walls, and a general sense of discomfort for me. So I set out at the beginning of the move on a mission. A mission, I assure you was a mission impossible. My mission was to get completely unpacked, get everything hung up on the walls, and have everything in its new, proper place within the first week. So when this incident happened, I was tired and well behind schedule.

In one final shout of desperation and frustration, I shouted a few choice words followed by, "My stupid dad! He didn't teach me how to do anything! And now I'm an useless idiot! I can't do anything!"

Of course in the heat of frustration, it only makes sense to blame someone else for my own shortcomings. After losing my temper on the floating shelves, I quit. I put down the remaining tools and parts I hadn't yet chucked across the room, and I fell to floor crying. I eventually got everything hung up and in its place, but not in the time frame I wanted. How could it be that I could become so frustrated from something as little as hanging a shelf?

I hate GPS

If there's one thing I hate, it's getting lost and spending more time en route somewhere than I need to. If I get turned around driving somewhere and it sets me back even a few minutes, I become so irritable you may anticipate me turning green and ripping my clothes off as my muscles morph into "The Hulk." I think it's because for me, I logically believe in this day and age, with GPS and all that jazz, you must be a fool if you get lost or turned around somewhere.

Well, when my wife and I moved to North Phoenix from southern Phoenix, there was a learning curve getting used to the streets. I was finally getting used to the roads and traffic patterns of where we had lived for a few years and now, I had to do it all over again. That frustrated me because it meant I had to rely on Mr. GPS for a lot of my directions. And Mr. GPS has not been a loyal companion in the past.

I had to head somewhere shortly after we had moved, and I had no clue how to get there. I decided to leave in plenty of time so I could take my time to find my destination. I entered the address correctly into the GPS and set sail. I was cruising along and all seemed to be going according to plan. However, there was a problem I was unaware of. In the location I was headed, the street name was a street that didn't run straight through. It was a street that was divided up by subdivisions and strip malls and would pick up somewhere else on the other end. And it would sometimes start back up randomly somewhere that wouldn't correlate geographically to where you would think it would start back up again. It was quite confusing, and I did not know about this. In the southern areas of Phoenix where we lived, everything was a nice, pretty grid. No tricks, no gimmicks. So you can imagine my surprise when my GPS started freaking out and re-routing every ten seconds trying to compensate for its terrible programming.

While the GPS was re-routing as fast as fat kids eat Popsicles, my brain was having its own technical difficulties. I began to feel a mixture of panic, anxiety, anger, and rage. I would make a turn, then have to go all the way around just to get past the median to make a U-turn, only to find out I needed to go the way I originally was going. Then after getting my directions correct, I would end up in a parking lot for an old abandoned Radio Shack. The GPS would tell me to turn on a road that didn't exist, because the names of the streets were different. All the while this is happening, I kept hearing that stupid British lady say, "Recalculating route." This is all because Apple iPhone developers decided to spend more time programming funny jokes, sayings, cuss words, and the best places to hide a dead body results into Siri than making sure their GPS was solid. If Steve Jobs was alive, I wouldn't have gotten lost, that's for sure.

Finally after reaching maximum Hulk status, I was literally starting to get dizzy. No joke. I was so angry I was getting dizzy. I needed to pull over and recollect myself before continuing. I pulled off into some rinky-dink parking lot where an abandoned Family Video and Long John Silvers used to be and I lost control. No cussing this time. My anger passed the cussing phase to maximum hulk status where words weren't even an option anymore. I clenched my fists so tight until my knuckles were white and my hands started to tingle. I tensed up my body as I took a deep breath. I locked my jaw, opened my eyes wide, and began to pound on the steering wheel with as much anger and strength I could muster up. At the same time, I released this gorilla scream at the top of my lungs. I wasn't saying anything. I was simply screaming until my throat was sore. I was in full-on rage mode. This proceeded for several minutes until my physical strength was depleted. And like the last story, when I was done, I rested my head on the steering wheel and wept like a baby.

Whose idea was this?!

The truth is, I'm not always great with discipline and challenges. I pride myself on my hard work, but it's always work I know how to do. I will spend countless hours cleaning, working in the yard and the garage, or on projects at work, but they are all things at which I would consider myself to be proficient. However, for some reason, when I'm faced a situation or a challenge that tests me beyond what I know or takes me to my limits of something I haven't mastered yet, I buckle. There's one more story that happened most recently, and it really sent a shockwave home for me.

This story's timeline is while Ashley and I are living in Kansas, and I'm pastoring a church. We had planned the first solid vacation together that didn't involve a major holiday like Christmas, or Thanksgiving, or someone getting married. The plan was to drive eighteen hours from Kansas to Pennsylvania to spend two whole weeks with my mom, step-dad, sisters, and lots more family. However, I now had a daughter, a dog, and my wife was pregnant with our son. Yes, we planned an eighteen-hour car ride with a pregnant woman, an eighteen-month-old toddler and a dog. It's like one of those decisions you wonder how in the world it ever got approved. For example: There is a tiny town in Oklahoma named Hooker. Yes. It is pronounced exactly how you are thinking it is. While driving through the town on the move to Kansas, we passed a sign for the Legion Baseball team and guess what their mascot was? The Horny Toads. Yep; they were the Hooker Horny Toads. No joke. In those situations, you can only wonder how in the world that name got approved. This car trip was similar. Who would allow the guy with apparent

Hulk-like tendencies on the road to drive eighteen hours with a pregnant woman, a dog, and a really strong-willed toddler?

Well, we got brave and decided to leave Kansas right after church services on a Sunday and drive straight through to Indianapolis for the night. Our plan was to drive the first ten hours on Sunday and the remaining eight hours on Monday. We figured we would be traveling several hours at night and wouldn't arrive in Indianapolis until midnight or later, so we knew it would be a good time to travel, so Aubrie could sleep a majority of it.

The drive took off without a hitch. Things were going swell. My wife and I were inhaling Taco Bell and singing Johnnyswim tunes while Aubrie and the dog napped. Things progressed and continued to be okay. After dinner, we knew Aubrie was getting tired, and we were looking forward to the last several hours in silence. As we left St. Louis, Aubrie finally fell asleep. With four more hours to go, we thought things were going to end perfectly.

What we didn't factor in the equation was Aubrie loves to toss and turn in her sleep. We had never taken a long road trip with Aubrie where she took more than a nap. Roughly around nine o'clock at night, Aubrie woke up to roll over, only to find herself strapped to a car seat unable to roll over. This made her very upset, and she began to cry. The crying got more intense and more severe until the crying turned into screaming. After a little bit more, it turned into that inconsolable scream/cry of a baby, when they aren't even coherent because they are so tired.

My daughter is strong-willed, which means there is no off button. She isn't one of those kids that will eventually wear themselves out screaming until they fall asleep. So Aubrie continued to scream and scream. In fact, we arrived in Indianapolis at one o'clock in the morning, and Aubrie was still screaming, non-stop. Ashley and I had been up since five-thirty in the morning on that Sunday and we were loopy to say the least. The irritation of a screaming baby was really getting to us.

I am convinced that if the police force and other units wanted more success in their interrogations, all they need to do is send them on an eighteen-hour car ride with a strong-willed child. Trust me, they'll talk.

As we began to get closer to Indianapolis, I got desperate to get relief from the screaming. Ashley was driving the last few hours for me, so I was in the passenger seat. I took my fingers like an elementary student, plugged my ears and put my head between my legs. It certainly helped with the screaming, but didn't help the perspective of my maturity.

When we arrived in Indianapolis, we were trying to find my little sister's apartment complex. She and my brother-in-law were gone on a missions trip, and we were just going to crash at their place over night. However, it was late, dark, and the street their apartment complex was on was a street with literally six or seven other apartment complexes strung along in a line, and none of them had their address displayed that we could see.

We think we find the right one and pull in the parking lot only to find out it's not the right one. We back out, and I'm frustrated at that point. My Hulk senses started to tingle. We pulled out and went down the road only to find out we went too far. Ashley pulled the car into some company's parking lot to turn around.

Now I pride myself when I say that up to this point in our

marriage, over four years, Ashley and I had never been in a fight. We have had arguments, but never fights. We have never said a single degrading word or term to each other. It was a goal we set for ourselves. I wouldn't even classify this as a fight, but some hurtful words were certainly said.

Aubrie is still screaming in an inconsolable way, both adults are really tired, and I don't like getting lost. As Ashley began to navigate back out of this company's parking lot, I threw my hands up in disgust. "You have got to be kidding me! This so stupid. This is ridiculous!" I shouted in a dramatic gesture.

And in a very pregnant, hormonal way, a very tired and irritable Ashley snipped back at me, "Shut up! Just shut up! Or I'm going to punch you in the face! I already have one crying baby in the back and I don't need another one! Just shut up!"

Needless to say, I shut up. I was in shock. That was the first time Ashley had said anything hurtful to me. We finally found the apartment, and when we got in we realized they had turned the air conditioning off in their apartment while on their missions trip to save money on their energy bill. It was a hot, muggy summer night in the Midwest and their apartment was a sticky eighty-nine degrees inside—a great way to add to the frustration.

The rest of the vacation went swell and we began our journey home with high hopes of a better trip back. We had fresh perspective and vowed to not speak to each other in a hurtful way again. On the trip home, Aubrie screamed nearly twelve of the eighteen hours. I'm not kidding or exaggerating. There were moments of desperation where we would pull over just to get out and stop the crying for ten minutes—even though we knew it would start up again as soon as we got back into the car.

I was becoming delusional and was anxiously thinking of ways to escape the madness. Remember, being in a car with a screaming baby for that long, any logic makes sense. In all seriousness, here's a thought process that went though my head. I was driving and I was next to a grass median. I figured I could potentially jump out of the car. Logically, it was okay because I would land on the shoulder of the road and roll into the grass median away from traffic. My plan was if I jumped out, I wouldn't die. But I would be injured enough from the velocity of hitting the pavement they would have to transport me to a hospital and eventually transport me home; thus getting me home without being trapped in a car with a screaming baby.

Transparent transition

I was trying to figure out why in the world I would get so upset over little things like hanging shelves and getting turned around on the road. I thought I figured it out and even blogged about it, but realized there's more to this than I initially thought. I don't struggle with normal anger issues. But it wasn't until that road trip to Pennsylvania the confirmation of my anger was screaming in my ear like my daughter.

Through these incidents, I realized something. All those situations and stories I shared with you were in seasons of life where I was amidst a major transition in my life. The first two stories with the shelves and the GPS were the same transition. My wife and I had established a life in the southern part of Phoenix, and then I decided to join a team in North Phoenix to plant a church. That season involved moving almost an hour north in Phoenix away from all family and friends, buying our first home and, since it was a church plant, we had to raise financial support like missionaries. There were a lot of unknowns in that season, and I like to control and plan my life. I couldn't do that with this particular season of life, and it caused me to live on the edge of anxiety and stress.

But it wasn't until that car ride when it really hit me. I looked at my life in that moment and didn't appear to be in too new of a season or transition. We had been in Kansas for almost two years, been in the same house since the day we moved, and life seemed pretty normal. Some of you may be thinking I'm over analyzing the car trip because who wouldn't be driven crazy in a car that long with a screaming baby? But I noticed it wasn't just the car ride. I was generally more weary, struggled with depression more than I did when my dad abandoned our family, and noticed I would get stressed and irritated more frequently.

And then it flashed in my mind like those flashing road signs: *Transitions make transparent the areas in our lives we are not trusting God fully.*

There was so much transition, it exposed how I wasn't fully trusting God to take care of things in His timing. I wanted to control everything and, when I couldn't, I got angry. Obviously I wasn't mad about the navigation mix up or the shelves. I was so stressed and fatigued from losing control of everything, I just exploded. It was the fact I wanted everything to go perfectly according to *my* plan and things rarely did. So I started to lose control, thus resulting in stress, anger, anxiety, and more.

The next time you have transition in your life, take a step back and look at what your transitions are making transparent about your life. And that's when I learned of my problem. I didn't appear to be in a specific transition when this road trip happened, but indeed I was. And it was the most difficult transition I had ever been a part of: I had become a *family man*.

You have to understand here, becoming a family man is a huge transition. I still remember when my daughter was born. It changed my life entirely. Life as I knew it was over. But at the same time, I had just begun a new life. A new life I was not expecting to change the way it did.

Don't wake me, I'm dreaming

There I sit on the back part of the wrap-around porch, first thing in the morning. Fresh, hot coffee that I roasted myself, laptop open, writing with a home run swing as the wrap-around porch overlooks the mountains and lakes of Colorado during sunrise. My golden retriever accompanies me on the porch, and my bank account is quite plentiful.

Sounds good, doesn't it? Unfortunately, it's just my imagination. I love my family, I love my life, and I feel blessed beyond belief. However, I have a confession to make. A sin for which I need to seek grace: *discontentment with my family*. While my life is wonderful, I often find myself day dreaming of a life that is full of my passions, beautiful scenery, financial sweatpants (comfortable), no need for a regimented job to provide for my family and, of course, no stress. A place where life is peaceful and doesn't include eighteen hour car rides with a screaming toddler.

Now enter my real life and the chaos ensues. Full-time job, interpersonal conflicts, dealing with annoying people, the fear of failure, a screaming baby with another one on the way, and a tight budget that screams even louder. Balancing my ever changing schedule while shuffling one car (we finally just got another one), grass that needs mowing, dishes that need done, bills that seem to show up at exactly the wrong time and, of course, barely any time to write. Oh yea, and that stupid dog that likes to use our house as his potty.

I used to write all the time. In fact, I used to write a lot of poetry, essays, memoirs, and even attempt writing the occasional song. But what happened? Why did it all stop or slow down to a near stop? Why have I had such writers' block? It's because I became a family man.

Don't try to hide it. We all day dream about simpler times with little to no responsibility, and sadly our minds categorize it as "better" times. But that's just it. I'm not just a man anymore. I'm a family man, which means I have a greater purpose. I have a beautiful wife to support, love, and cherish. I have an adorable, precious daughter, and a handsome son to care for and raise in a Godly manner. I have a job I love, so I strive to do the best I can, and I have ministries to lead. And my number one ministry is my family.

While my imagination is great, and the scenario on the deck would be great, I have a greater purpose than writing and drinking coffee. Becoming a family man has been a difficult transition for me, but it's only going to make me a better man. In fact it's a good simulation to Christ's love for us. I sacrifice personal time,

I sacrifice dreams, I sacrifice money, and I sacrifice emotions on my family instead of selfish desires. As parents, we are called to live outside ourselves and serve. When you do, God will bless you.

Maybe he'll bless me with a vacation for a week to live out that dream on a deck in Colorado, but in the meantime, I recognize that I could fulfill personal happiness or I could be filled with joy: an everlasting joy of serving your family even when it's inconvenient. Trust me, when I walk my daughter down the aisle on the day of her wedding, knowing that I raised her in the most godly way possible, and I give her hand to the man I trust to take care for her for the rest of her life, that will be better than any cup of coffee I could ever make or any sentence I could ever write. And that's worth sticking around for.

RUNNING

I started "running" recently. If you know me at all, you are either really impressed or you literally just laughed out loud at the thought of me doing that. Usually, I only embrace this stupid thing called running in only two life events.

One: *If someone is chasing me and trying to kill me.* Even then, my running is limited. Honestly, if someone is actually chasing me, trying to kill me, I either deserve it, or it's natural selection at its best.

And two: *If there's a spider.* This one happens more frequently and usually involves me running from one part of the house to another to inform my wife she has to go kill a spider.

My running—and I should use air quotes every time I use the word—is not at all like one of those guys in triathlons. No, no. My running is almost equivalent to a walrus ironing clothes. I mean, he could probably do it, but it wouldn't look much like ironing. You would get a good laugh out of it, and you would applaud and encourage him in his valiant attempt anyway because, come on, it's a walrus ironing clothes. That's pretty impressive all on its own. I use running as a reference point for something I am attempting to do.

I am a bigger guy. I would say I am fat, but others would probably consider me husky or stalky, but I know what they're really thinking. I have a big chest, broad shoulders, a thick neck, and a full face. My legs are short and like tree trunks. My dad was a short body-builder, and I apparently lost the gene pool and got his. I also have pretty intense asthma and poor sinuses, so the idea of me running is just an image I wish upon no one. Unless it's between a picture of me running or me in a Speedo. Then I would wish you would see a picture of me running.

Next time, I'll just watch the movie

A worship leader acquaintance of mine made a video. He has a similar build to me, and I'm pretty sure he even weighed a bit more than me. In this video for a church he is a part of, he explains how he started running and how it has impacted his life. Frustrated with my own exercise disciplines, I thought about running. I figured if he could do it, I could too. So I decided to run.

I didn't even know where to start with the actual execution of running. So I did what any twenty-first century person would do. I downloaded an app for my phone. The app was rated really high and did lots of things. It had a GPS to map my routes, clocked my times, counted my calories, and told me how far I was going—all in a cool British accent.

I didn't have a plan. I didn't have a goal. In fact, I was more convinced I was going to have to go to the ER after a neighbor found me passed out around the block from my asthma. I figured I would put on some good tunes and just run. If I only got down the street and back, I would be okay with that. My problem with fitness goals is I never achieve them or at least not in the time frame I want to; essentially always setting myself up for failure. Not this time. I knew it would be a miracle to get around the block. So I set my expectations low, embarrassingly low. I decided I would just run. Nothing else; simply run. And that's exactly what I did.

The next morning, I woke up early. I put on my exercise shorts and my sneakers that were surely not designed for running—I'm assured of that now. I then grabbed my phone, my inhaler, and walked out the front door.

I set low expectations for myself but honestly, what I expected from my experience was the scene from the movie *Rocky II* where he trains for his fight. There's an epic running scene that starts with Rocky looking in on his son's crib. Then he busts out the front door simultaneously leaping over the front staircase railing and takes off like a super hero. He runs past trains and dominates the train tracks. Then he hits the streets and marketplaces of downtown Philadelphia. Because of his popularity, as he runs people shout his name and cheer him on all while he loses no momentum. Then as he turns a corner, there is a mob of children who excitedly chase him. Rocky slows down in kindness to allow the kids to be able to keep up with him. The further he runs, the more kids start to run with him. Then in a feat of passion, he begins to hurdle a series of benches in a park and the kids are amazed. As he hits the main drag on Benjamin Franklin Parkway, he begins to pick up speed and starts to lose the mob of hundreds of kids. As the final kid to keep up with him begins to trail off, you hear the kid scream, "Go! Go! Go! Go! Gooooo!," to which Rocky, like lightening, runs up the stairs of the Philadelphia Museum of Art, and as he crests the top of the staircase, he begins to celebrate as the child mob catches back up to him and all shout in unison, "Rocky!" numerous times. It was a glorious scene, and it played in the back of my mind as I looked in on my daughter's crib before I left. Low expectations, huh?

Here's what really happened. I bolted out the front door and immediately stopped. I contemplated leaping over the stone wall on our front staircase, but realized I couldn't leap that high. I walked down our front staircase and started to "run." I had to stop multiple times to use my inhaler, and my earbuds kept falling out because I sweat so much the sweat went into my ears causing them to slip out. People driving by probably thought I was injured by the way I was running. I looked to be in severe pain. By the end of the run, I was at a pace equivalent to a senior citizen rushing to the senior citizen discount buffet, and there was no mob of kids following me. I think what set me back the most from running like Rocky Balboa was the cool headband and sweat suit he wore.

———————

But I did it. I "ran." In fact I made it 1.85 miles. I was blown away at my success. I was literally soaked with sweat and I could barely breathe, but I did it. In fact I have continued running multiple days a week since that first run. I feel accomplished, and now I feel credible enough to take the quotations off the word.

Running has been a liberating experience for me. I actually enjoy doing it. It is the most painful thing I've ever done exercise wise, and while I'm doing it, it hurts so bad. My feet hurt, my joints ache, and I hate how early I have to get up to do it. But when I get back; when I'm done, I get this rush. Some say it's probably what they call the "runners high," but whatever it is, it feels good. I feel awake, alert and confident.

I actually notice a difference in my productivity on the days that I run and the days that I don't. And I think I've figured out why.

It's because I'm not a runner. Most people wouldn't classify me in that category. I have asthma and sinus issues, I have a husky build, and I'm not athletic. Yet, I did it. I conquered the challenge. I not only ran, but I ran two miles and even more now! My productivity comes from that confidence. The confidence that comes from conquering something towering you. For me, I am motivated and confident to take on the world and all its challenges for the day because I already conquered one of the toughest things for me, personally. I start my day with the most difficult thing I'll probably encounter for the day, so I know if I can run at least a minimum of two miles with these lungs, then I can do anything.

Nature or nurture

My daddy didn't teach me much about life. And before you start classifying him as a deadbeat dad, let me explain. My dad was fun and funny. He could lift a lot of weight, and he taught me everything I needed to know about sports. He taught me how to hate the Pittsburgh Steelers really well. My love for hockey and football is because of him. He wasn't a deadbeat dad. He was a good dad when we were young. What he didn't teach me, though, were the things I needed to be a man in this world. And it wasn't because he was mean and didn't want to teach me. I'm convinced it was because he simply didn't know how.

I struggle with a lot of insecurities, and you probably already know that by now. One of them I still struggle with is the inability to know how to do things. I know guys that can fix anything, build anything, or remodel anything—and I've never been taught how to change a tire on my car. In fact, at the age of twenty-six, I still didn't know how to change a tire. I was getting ready to leave on a road trip, and I shared with my lead pastor (my boss) about my anxiety of a road trip and how I was afraid of a flat tire because I didn't know how to change it. What if it went flat in the middle of nowhere with no cell signal to call anyone? What would I do? So he offered to show me how.

I still have the guys at the auto store change my windshield wipers for me, because I don't know how. Something simple goes wrong with my toilet, I call a plumber. In fact, I know so little that while living in Kansas, something went wrong with our stove-top burner and the first person my wife called was her dad. At first it made me mad she didn't call me first, but then I realized that I would have just ended up calling him anyway because I wouldn't know how to fix it and my father in-law can fix anything. Seriously. One time my wife's hair straightener broke, and he took it apart, and re-wired it, or whatever he did, and fixed it.

But that's simply the way my father in-law is. I used to think there was literally nothing he couldn't fix. Then we had our daughter, and she decided to see how hard she could throw our television remote onto the wood floor. No worries, grandpa was coming for a visit soon, so he would fix it. After a great attempt, he handed us the remote, and simply said he couldn't fix it. (Leave it up to my daughter to damage something so badly that it is beyond his ability to repair.)

It used to really bug me when we lived in Phoenix that anything we needed repaired on our house would entail me calling my father in-law over to fix. I thought once we moved to Kansas, that would go away, but it didn't. It just meant instead of having to wait a week for him to come fix it, we now have to wait until his next visit to Kansas. I used to beat myself up for having him fix everything until I realized that my father in-law is actually the bi-product of the opposite end of the spectrum of life from me. My father in-law knows so much for two reasons: he's a seasoned engineer and his dad.

Ashley's grandpa was such an incredible man. He was so incredible, I think God took him from us early to heaven because God realized how much of an asset Grandpa was and probably figured He certainly wanted a guy like Grandpa with Him. Ashley's grandpa was a real man. He was an incredible father, a great, loving husband who cherished his wife, worked super hard, and knew how to wear aviator sunglasses no matter the decade and make it look cool. There was nothing that outmatched that man's drive and work ethic, except for his wife's ability to cook.

The Ugly Couch

When Grandpa was young, he needed a job. He heard of a job opening that could pay well to do roofing, or siding, or something in that category. He had never done it a day in his life and didn't know the first thing about it. He walked in and requested the job. They asked him if he had any roofing/siding experience. He said yes, and that he had a lot of experience. They gave him the job. His first day on the job, he simply watched them do the job for a little bit and jumped right in. I'm sure he didn't have it right or perfect in the first attempt or even the second attempt. But no kidding, the end of the first day, he was the fastest roofer/sider on the team.

In their many years together, Ashley's grandpa and grandma purchased many houses and flipped them. They took regular homes and remodeled them to be luxurious. Grandpa did all the work himself with some minimal hired help. If he thought, *Hey I think it would look cool if that wall was gone*, he wouldn't blueprint it out or strategize a plan; he would just tear the wall down.

Shortly before his passing, as a retired man, he was bored and decided he should do marketing for his local Chamber of Commerce—with absolutely no experience. I'm pretty sure they didn't even have a position for it. He walked in and told them why they needed to hire him to do marketing for them. He convinced them—and they hired him.

That seemed to be a trend with Grandpa. He would just simply do it, despite the lack of knowledge or experience, and learn on the way. My father in-law got that from him. Because of Grandpa, my father in-law was taught all of these incredible things. Of all the things his dad taught him, the one that I find the most valuable, is the confidence to just do something without fear. Don't know how to do it? That's okay. Google it or just figure it out on the way.

Now that I'm a husband, father, and homeowner, I get really prideful when I have to ask for help. Especially if it's something I feel like I should know how to do.

I have this tendency to pass off the things I don't know how to do and blame others for my insufficiencies. I have moments of severe frustrations at my dad for not teaching me the things it takes to take care of a car or a house. The reality is that my father in-law learned because he had a father teach him. My dad didn't teach me the things I needed, but I also know his dad didn't teach him those things either.

Excuse my excuses

I'm not great at many things, but one thing I'm good at is making excuses. I always have one hundred reasons why I can't do something. I think it's because I'm a good salesman. My mom always told me I was either the world's best salesman or I would break a record for being full of the most BS. And if you don't know what BS means, I'm sorry you're so sheltered. I can't tell you here what it means because this is a Christian book, so just Google it.

See, a lot of this is my own doing. Sure I could blame my dad all day for the things I can't do, but that would be like President Obama blaming President Bush for being a terrible president, and he would never do that. I tend to fear failure in everything. So, if I'm not 100 percent confident in what I'm doing, I tend to make excuses to get out of it so I don't run the risk of failing.

Let's look at a real life situation here. I can't make this stuff up. This literally just happened as I sat here writing this chapter. Let me take you back to this morning. My wife asks me to take the title of our new vehicle to the tag office to get our license plate. I say okay, but I'm nervous about it. Nervous about going to get a license plate? Yea I know, I'm crazy. But I'm nervous because I'm not 100 percent sure where the building is, how to do it, or what documents to bring with me. I'm afraid of looking stupid in the tag office for not having the proper documents. As a man, I should know how to do something so small, simple, and stupid like going to the tag office.

So this afternoon, I planned to head to the tag office, then to Starbucks to get out of the house for a little bit and get some writing done. I exited the house through the garage to take the vehicle that needed the tag. In a last second psych out, I convinced myself that I would have certainly forgot something and would surely look like a fool in front of everyone at the tag office. So I took the other car instead and headed straight to Starbucks. I figured I would come up with some excuse, like the childcare kid's car seat was still in the vehicle, to tell my wife as to why I didn't take the new vehicle to get a tag.

It's not even that big of a deal honestly. So what if I took the wrong papers or did it wrong? They would tell me the right documents to bring, and everything would okay. But I was still afraid to fail, so I came up with an excuse and just didn't do it.

Another example: *laundry*. My mother has been showing me how to do laundry for years, but I still make up excuses to not do it. Why? Because I'm afraid to fail. I'm afraid I'll mess up and cause one of my favorite shirts to shrink or turn my favorite shirt pink by washing it with something I'm not supposed to.

Sure, I don't know how to do a lot of things, but I also don't give myself the opportunity to learn because of my excuses. My fear of failure disables me from learning and growing.

The grass is greener because I made it green

I'm still a work in progress, but I've been getting better. I've been forcing myself to take on challenges and just figure them out as I go. Especially at my church job, I do lots of projects and things that I start and have no clue how to execute or sustain, but I simply start them. I start them because if I do, then I have to finish them. Also, because if I don't start them, my fear of failure will convince me to never start them.

Last year, I was sick of dirt, rock, and weeds as my front yard and longed for a lush green front lawn. I had no idea what to do, but decided to do it anyway. I grew up in Pennsylvania, where it is green naturally. You just had grass whether you wanted it or not. So nurturing a lawn was new to me. What if I put a ton of work into it and the grass doesn't grow? I didn't let that fear cripple my dream. I Googled suggestions on starting a new yard and began. I couldn't afford a tiller, so I went outside on a really hot day with a garden hoe and started chopping up my front lawn. It wasn't too long into the project that I had wished I hadn't started the project as my arms started to hurt. My neighbor came out and asked me if I would like to use a tiller. I told him of course, but couldn't afford one. He told me his grandfather had one I could use. Things began to look up.

That day, I spent eight solid hours outside tearing up my

yard into loose dirt that I then seeded and fertilized. Everyday for the next two months, I watered it a couple times a day until my yard was green. But, I didn't quite get what I expected.

I didn't get that lush green lawn I wanted. My yard was still young and my soil composition was bad (something I learned from Google). So my yard was green and full of grass, but it just wasn't thick and it was a bit spotty. I kept working on it until winter hit and the snow made it go dormant. Once spring had sprung, I re-seeded, re-fertilized and began the hard work again. Except this time it was a bit different. My yard still wasn't what I wanted, but it was better than the previous year. It was super dark green and had filled in really nicely. I've continued to work on it all summer and I know, come fall, I will need to re-seed again.

But what's encouraging me is the fact that there's progress. I put in tons of work and didn't get the result I wanted, but I got a result. So I continued to work hard on it and now, little by little, I'm seeing progress. Come next spring, my yard will be in even better shape. But I won't have achieved it in one season. It's taken multiple seasons to turn the bad soil composition into something that is full of rich nutrients. But I would have never gotten my yard at all if I lived in my excuse world. The fact that I just did it, despite not knowing, forced me to grow and learn. Now I have something I'm proud of.

A running faith

We need to learn to embrace life, and our faith like my running. Some of us never run or did at one point and stopped. A lot of us make excuses—we are pretty good at it. And honestly, some of the excuses are legitimate. Some of us have hindrances that put us in a position to think we can't run. But what if the best medicine for our hindrances is the very thing we're hindered to do?

See, I started to run and I'm proud of that. But what I didn't tell you, and what I chose to ignore my entire life, was that the doctors told me at a very young age the best medicine for my asthma was running. They told me if I ran a lot, eventually my lungs would grow stronger, outlasting my asthma. Instead, I ✳ chose to ignore it and use my asthma as an excuse to never run. I chose to live a life not running, *with* asthma because I didn't want to endure the pain or possible failure in it. My hindrance to running was actually the best medicine for my lungs. Go figure.

You may not think you're a runner. In fact you may feel hindered to run because of your bad lungs. You may even use it as an excuse or come up with an even better excuse to not run.

You don't have to live inside your weaknesses. Your weaknesses don't have to define you. In fact, how often do our weaknesses in turn make us stronger?

Like Ashley's grandpa, I can live life thinking the Chamber of Commerce could use a marketing guy but never do anything about it because I'm not an expert in marketing. Or I can walk in and tell them why they need me. I can be afraid to do laundry for the rest of my life in fear of ruining one of my favorite shirts or just do it. And when I do ruin a shirt, realize it's not the end of the world and buy a new shirt. And just to clarify, I do laundry now. I'm not that pathetic anymore.

Sure, I don't know how to fix a water leak in my house or change the oil in my car. I can live in that weakness as an excuse

✳ HEALING ON THE SABBATH / WOH

to not live a good life or I can run. I can jump in with no plan and just do it, learning on the way.

Working on my yard that first day was so much work. I was sun burnt, I was sore, I was tired, I felt weak, and the work didn't stop. I had to continue to labor on my yard daily. But it got easier, and I felt so confident for accomplishing something that I had no idea I could even do.

My dad's dad didn't teach him things. Now, I can blame my dad for all my weaknesses and for not teaching me how to do things, or...I can run. I can choose to follow another pattern. Because if I don't, I won't have anything to teach my son.

We need to embrace life and faith like my running. Running doesn't need a plan. Just do it. Go as far as you can. It's going to be painful, it's not going to be pretty. It may even look like a walrus ironing clothes. But when your covered in sweat, catching your breath with sore knees, you'll get that runners' high and realize it's worth the pain. Choose to run with your life, not sit in the excuse-filled asthma world. And remember your weaknesses are actually the things that will make you stronger in the long run (pun intended).

THE PERFECT

SIGNIFICANCE

One evening, I was walking through Walmart doing what I do best: browsing the home and décor sections wishing I could buy everything. I may have overdosed on smells that night—I smelled every single candle on the shelf. But amidst my perusing, I saw this lady pushing a cart with a fold out lawn chair and a blanket in her cart. Maybe she needed them so she could watch her son's soccer game or maybe she was preparing for a family picnic. Then I started thinking about how I wanted a chair. I didn't need a chair, but now I wanted one. As I contemplated which color of chair I wanted, I realized something: *it was Thanksgiving evening.* That meant that Black Friday shopping was creeping in quickly and chaos was soon to ensue. Being awakened to this realization spun me into an episode of the *Twilight Zone* as I continued to watch this lady with her cart. She was indeed buying those items to prepare. But it surely wasn't for her son's soccer game. In fact, she went into Walmart to buy a lawn chair and blanket so she could sit outside Walmart for five hours in line for the midnight sale. Yes, this lady literally purchased these items so she could sit in line to buy more things. As I walked out of the store to affirm my observations, I got to see a massive line anticipating this midnight sale. It seemed counter-productive that the money she would probably save from this midnight sale, she had just spent on a chair and a blanket.

A perfect perfectionist

The word perfection is an interesting one at that. The more I reflect and ponder the defining characteristics of the word and its usage, the more I realize it's the most imperfect word there is.

We use the word perfection to define all sorts of things. In music, we talk about perfect pitch, perfect fifths, and perfect fourths. With food and drink, we claim that lattes are made perfectly, or that steaks are grilled to perfection. In athletics, the quarterback threw a perfect precision pass and that basketball player's shots were perfectly aligned with the hoop.

One day as I was thinking about the word perfection, I decided to do a scientific study. So I Googled what the word perfection meant to the general Internet. Some of the defining characteristics of perfection that I discovered were: without flaw, unbreakable structures, endless joy, love, creation, and some chemistry thing I don't remember.

In every element of our lives we have a measuring stick for perfection, and it's usually all in regard to the variables involved. And based on the answers I got from Google, you can see that. Love? How is love perfect? Is there even an unbreakable structure that exists? Creation? We are so messed up as a people and world, how is that perfect? That basketball player's shots were perfect compared to what? Who is determining the perfect nature of your latte? Is there a committee that sits in a room and tests these things? Maybe it's the same committee of dentists, where nine of them seem to all recommend the same toothpastes; except that one dentist. He always disagrees with the other nine in every toothpaste commercial. They should fire him and hire me. I'd love to test toothpastes and lattes.

That's what makes the word perfection so interchangeable and overused. We don't truly understand perfection, and yet we all hold ourselves to that standard. We pursue perfection, knowing full well, that we cannot be perfect. That basketball player cannot possibly shoot perfectly. At some point, he is going to over rotate his shot by the slightest percent. On a musical scale, you cannot sing every single note absolutely perfect every single time.

So as we go about our days, we stumble through them, beating ourselves up because we are not perfect. In fact, we encourage it. It's quite a sad fact that in the game of professional football, if a starting quarterback—the face of the team and organization—throws an imperfect pass, he is immediately on the chopping block for his job. He gets paid millions of dollars to throw perfect passes, so he better not mess up. The reality is that he is going to throw bad passes and lots of them, because he is not perfect. We go to restaurants and criticize the chef because the steak we wanted came slightly a little more pink than we requested. We paid a lot of money for our steak, and that chef needs to get it right. This is flawed logic because the chef isn't perfect and neither is his equipment. Humans are not perfect and humans make grills. Which means grills cannot be perfect. His grill cannot cook the exact same way every time.

————————————

Unfortunately, perfection has become all relative to the lens of our perspective. With such a misguided view on perfection, we then begin to look at our spiritual lives in a way that is destined to have a misguided approach.

When looking at Scripture, what's the most pressing thing for us to pursue on this side of eternity? Holiness. So Christians attempt holiness; some of us more than others. But somewhere in our attempts and pursuits of holiness, we have managed to change the measuring stick we use. Like I said before, perfection is measured usually by the variables involved. And in our pursuit of holiness, we have managed to eliminate the most important variable: God. We begin to compare our holiness to everyone and everything else. Our measuring stick for holiness becomes society. Don't get me wrong, living a holy life compared to society is important and valuable, but it shouldn't be the measuring stick we use.

Actually Scripture talks about this fairly explicitly. Romans 13 and Titus 1:5-9, just to name a few, talk candidly about living "above reproach," living a holy and blameless life. (These Scriptures refer directly to those who want to hold a major leadership position in the church). But here's where it gets interesting. In those passages, Paul, the author, speaks of living a holy life on earth and the importance of it, yet in Romans 7:13-25, he makes the statement, "Oh what a wretched man I am! Who will save me from this body of death?!" So Paul spends many, many verses talking about living a good life, yet he calls himself a wretched man. Confused yet? Paul is referencing the real measuring stick for holiness: *God.*

We are called to live pure and holy lives here on this earth. That is true. But when we step back and look at holiness, it's all relative to who we are comparing it to. Yeah to society, we may look real good. We brush our shoulders off and think we are good. When asked if we drink alcohol, we puff our chests out and proudly proclaim that "We do not!" We brag about our convictions and talk about how full our iPods are of Casting Crowns and Chris Tomlin tunes. Our favorite movies are Christian movies like *Fireproof* and the *Left Behind* series, and we turn any movie off after the second cuss word. One cuss is okay, but two . . . now that's the line. And don't forget that we weren't sexually active before marriage. You gotta boast about that. Otherwise, what was the point? And subconsciously we debate the authenticity of people's faith who don't live this way; especially those "Christians" who vote Democrat. But I vote Republican, because I want to go to heaven.

Of course all of these things aren't bad things to uphold. It's a great thing to not be consumed with alcohol and to keep your mind pure of the movies and music you listen to, but these aren't the things that define our holiness. To society we may look like angels, but when we step back and compare our holiness to God's holiness we realize just how wretched we are. See the difference? When we have a true fear of the Lord, we will view our lives in regards to God's holiness, not to the rest of the world.

God's holiness

When we compare our lives and holiness to God, it affects our worship in a way that is unexplainable. We look up and recognize the power and majesty, and we cannot help but fall to our knees in worship. But that's not what we do. We have built our faith and spirituality around Bible studies, Sunday programs, and living under this dome of Christendom.

We simply look at God as a vitamin to whatever deficiency we have in our lives. Need God to help with our finances? Get a glass of water and pop a couple of "God is provision" pills and we'll be good. We brand God as the *doctor* or *healer* and slap His sacred image to it. Or we take the word *love* and slap God's sacred image to it. But that's not *all* God is. That is such a small, unrealistic view. Those are mere attributes. God is majestic, so pure and holy you would literally crumble in His presence.

When we compare our holiness to anything other than the Lord, we have such a small misguided view of holiness. But when we view our holiness to God's holiness, we get the blessing of guilt. And this is where living a good life comes as a bi-product.

There are two kinds of guilt that I'll talk about here. There is a guilt that simply looks to ourselves or there is guilt that looks to Jesus. The guilt that looks to us is what I like to call "shame guilt" and the second kind of guilt is more commonly known as "conviction guilt." Shame guilt looks to ourselves and doesn't care necessarily about holiness. Usually, shame guilt is a guilt built around feeling bad. We feel bad because we got caught or got in trouble. But conviction guilt looks to Jesus.

Conviction guilt grieves the lack of holiness in our lives. We realize how wretched we are in comparison to God's holiness. True conviction reveals a heart that can recognize sin. We can see the areas we are falling short of God's throne. Conviction calls us to action and change; shame causes us to hide.

Full circle

This all came full circle for me in my life. I always thought I had a pretty good perspective on God and who He was, but with such misguided views of holiness and perfection, I certainly didn't.

On January 12, 2013, at 6:23 p.m., I finally saw who God was in His perfection. And no, that wasn't the day I got my haircut, even though my hair is awesome all the time; especially on haircut day. That was the day my first child was born.

Growing up, I was taught who God was and how to view Him. I was told to view Him as *King, healer, friend,* and *father.* I was taught names like *Abba, Heavenly Father* and, of course, the simple, *Dad.* And that was where I got stuck. I knew that in Galatians 4:6 it says, "And because you are sons, God has sent the Spirit of his Son into our hearts, crying, "Abba! Father!" I understood the imagery well, but I couldn't fully grasp it. I couldn't grasp the significance of it. In a society where the majority of children live fatherless or abandoned, why in the world would I embrace God as a father?

During the times of my life without a godly father figure, people would try to encourage me and say things like, "Don't worry because your real father is always with you," or "Your heavenly father would never leave you." All valid truths, except again, I found myself confused and perplexed at the situation. I could understand the significance, but I couldn't grasp it.

As I basked in the joy of my daughter's birth, I witnessed it. I witnessed perfection. I felt an adoration and love for her and tears could express only a small amount of what I was feeling.

Now I feel I have a whole new level of understanding of God's love for us. I now understand the significance and amount of love He has for us when He calls us sons and daughters in 2 Corinthians.

One of my favorite memories of my daughter's infancy was when I would kick back on the recliner and lay my daughter on my chest. I never felt closer to my daughter than when I laid her on my chest. The crazy part about it was she didn't know it. She didn't understand it. She couldn't grasp the significance. Yet, regardless of whether she could reciprocate that love, I still held her close to my chest.

This is what God does to us. He draws near to us even in the times we don't understand it or know it. Even when we cannot reciprocate it, He still lays us on His chest. Now imagine how much more amazing it could be if we understood His love for us and could reciprocate it. Imagine if we could fully grasp where our heads are laying!

Perfect passion

I can only assume the lady waiting in line outside of Walmart was full of passion and excitement. Excited for whatever sale she was attempting to capitalize on. It must have been a valuable product, because I wouldn't go through what this lady went through, wait in line that long just to purchase something small like shampoo. Then again, maybe I would. I guess it would depend on how many people were smelling my hair on a regular basis. At this moment though, I don't have people flocking to me to smell my hair.

This lady understood the significance the item she was going to purchase would play in her life. Maybe it was a large, high-definition television that would significantly increase the enjoyment of binge watching shows on Netflix. Maybe it was the newest video game system that would make her "Mother of the Year" to her son. She understood the significance and embraced it with everything she had, to the point it cost her something.

When we can understand God's love for us, and fully grasp the significance of it, I bet our relationship with Christ will change dramatically. God wants us to draw near to Him, and if we can realize where our heads are laying, we can stop running around focusing on trying to live perfect lives here on earth and embrace Him with everything we have.

This is where we all need to land. It's not that we need to be perfect. It's not even about living a more holy life than the guy you work with. We recognize God is our father and we strive to live holy lives in the same way a child models their parents. It's about the pursuit, not the perfect results. God cares that we love Him and embrace Him. That we run to His arms and understand He is holy—and we are not. What if we pursued God and His holiness with the same excitement as the lady who ran into the arms of consumerism on Black Friday?

When imperfect people try to measure perfection, the significance of perfection can only be watered down to our capability to execute it. But when we grasp where our heads are truly laying, we are able to recognize the significance of God's love in our lives is the perfection we need to cling to.

THE BORDER OF KANSAS

I've been addicted to coffee since I was twelve years old. My affinity for coffee began as just a young cub. I remember vividly sneaking tastes of my father's coffee. My dad had a tendency to have a cup of coffee while sitting in the big comfy couch-chair thing we had, while he watched ESPN. He would habitually sit his coffee up on the floor next to the chair and leave it there. To my benefit, there was always about a half-inch or so of coffee remaining. I would usually find it the next morning, and I would take his cup of cold, leftover coffee and drink it. It was glorious.

My favorite thing about drinking the cold, leftover coffee was how sweet it was. My dad was king of sugar in his coffee. The amounts of sugar he consumed in a single cup was astonishing. Medically, I don't want to know how bad that was for me and especially him. All I know, is that it tasted fantastic.

It was then I realized how much I liked coffee. I'm sure the sugar had a lot to do with it, but it was the sugar *in* coffee specifically I loved. My dad taught me how to make the sweetest, best tasting cup of coffee. By the age of twelve, I was having a cup daily with my dad. As I got older, I decided to venture out and try my coffee *straight*, with nothing in it, and eventually I graduated myself to the wonderful world of espresso. At this current point in my life, I average at least a pot of coffee a day. I even journeyed so far as to start roasting my own coffee.

There's just so much I love about coffee. I love that distinguishing smell in the morning that gets my brain awake. I thoroughly enjoy the butt-kicking, punch-you-in-the-face, first sip in the morning. I love the texture of the coffee beans. I love hearing that sound of the grinder grinding up the beans. When making a pour-over cup of coffee, I love creating the flume with the grinds and water. I love tasting different flavor notes such as: *acidity, nutty, fruity, herbal* and more. I love lattes and the froth. I love the *crema* with the pouring of espresso. I love the feeling of holding a warm ceramic coffee mug in my hand. It's my sense of comfort. I don't just like coffee or drink it, it's a part of my life. I can't imagine a life without it; nor do I even want to.

Coffee isn't about the initial taste, it's about the experience. For me, coffee isn't just a beverage; it's a part of me. With coffee, I don't consume it, I'm consumed *by* it.

Ohio roads are terrible

My wife and I used to have a long-distance relationship. I was living at home in Pennsylvania going to school, and Ashley was still at school in Indiana. About once a month, I would make the seven-hour drive from Pennsylvania to Indiana to visit her for a weekend. The drive was so distinguishable depending on which state I was in. Pennsylvania was always so beautiful: trees, ridge lines, rolling hills, and so much green. But it was always so obvious when I crossed the boarder from Pennsylvania to Ohio. The Ohio highways are just awful. They are old, torn up, and terribly worn down. It is flat, brown, and filled with corn fields. I'm not officially making a statement about Ohio, but I just want to point out, I saw a bumper sticker once that said, "Ohio is the state God forgot to finish."

The point though, is it was obvious when I was no longer in Pennsylvania. Now I'm not suggesting Pennsylvania is better that Ohio, I'm just saying at least we have trees, and good sports teams, and cities people actually want to go to. Oh, and Yuengling beer. I'm just pointing out the facts here, people. Just like it's a fact the only good thing Ohio had left were the old Lebron James jerseys, and now they don't even have those because they burned them all when he left Cleveland the first time.

I knew the moment I felt the condition of the highway change under my tires, I was in for the long, lame, portion of my drive through Ohio. This portion was three hundred miles or so of my four hundred and fifty mile travel time. It was long, flat, and miserable. Even the cows looked depressed.

But what's interesting to me are the states that look the same at the borders. You know, the states that look identical at the border, and the only thing that distinguishes them from each other is the states' "Welcome" sign. How did they decide that specific spot was going to be the border? There are several states like this, but there is one border that intrigues me the most. It's the border of Kansas and Colorado.

The Ugly Couch

I hear people talk about Colorado all the time, and I've seen some stunning pictures: gorgeous snow-capped mountains with lush pine trees, calming lakes, rivers, and more. I've never been to Colorado technically, but I have to been to the border of Kansas and Colorado, and it's nothing like that.

Living in Kansas currently, I understand the joke about Kansas: if you've seen one square mile of Kansas, you've seen it all. So it shocked me when I had the opportunity to go to the border of Kansas and Colorado. I wasn't expecting the mountains to literally be at the border, but I guess I just expected more. There was absolutely no difference between the two states at the border. The only thing separating the two was a sign. My perspective was shattered.

Why wouldn't they just make the border when it starts to look cool? If I had to base a trip to Colorado on the initial perceptive, I would be sadly disappointed. But the kicker for me, was I knew what Colorado really had in store. I'd seen the pictures, heard the stories. I knew if you kept driving, deep into the state of Colorado, the scenery would change. It would change, because the farther you drove into Colorado, the more you were separating yourself from Kansas. Then, after venturing deep into Colorado, the pictures would come to life and the stories would become a reality.

There's a point when you don't need a sign to tell you you're in Colorado; you just know. You see the lakes, you see the mountains, you can smell the trees, and you can see the anti-meat eating, hippie people riding bikes wearing homemade clothes. You know you're in Colorado not because a sign told you, but because the scenery makes it abundantly clear.

Halloween candy and shoes

There's one holiday that just baffles me. It's Halloween; I just don't get it. Now on the surface it makes sense: you dress up in a costume, take a bag, and go knocking on peoples doors hoping they'll give you candy. And if you're particularly lucky, some creepy guy with pet tarantulas won't poison the candy. If you're unlucky, you'll end up at the activist mother's house who is protesting Halloween because of health and religious convictions and you'll end up with a toothbrush and a pamphlet telling you heaven is better than Snickers.

What I don't get, on a deeper level, is why we go through all this effort for Kit-Kat bars. Look at the logic: your parents buy a bunch of candy. Like seriously, a years supply of it to hand out to the Trick or Treaters yet, in order for you to get candy, you have to dress up like Dan Marino or Elsa and walk like two miles around town. Why don't your parents just buy you a bunch of candy? Now that makes sense.

Because of the flawed logic of getting candy on Halloween, this resulted in lazy Trick or Treating in my older, middle school to high school years. I would find the easiest costumes I could possibly find and beg for candy. I used to have a newspaper route, so one year I threw my paper bag over my shoulder and went as a paper boy. It was a clutch costume, because it was just a bag, but the bag as the costume also doubled as the candy holder. Another year I put on one of those "Hello My Name Is" stickers and told people I was a visitor. Another year, I just took my Bible and went as a Christian.

———————

Basically, I wanted all the benefits of Halloween—like non-poisoned candy and no toothbrushes—but didn't want to jump in and participate in the experience. It also reminds me of generic shoe brands. My family growing up didn't have very much money. That meant pizza and a two liter once a month as a treat, I got a PlayStation 1 when the Playstation 2 came out, and that certainly meant no name brand clothes.

Nowadays, the brand on the clothes mean literally nothing to me. Unless it's Express. I love Express clothing. But as a kid and teenager, the brands of your clothing meant everything. On the first day of school, all the kids would come in sporting the coolest new Nike or Adidas shoes and I would be sporting some Mexican rip-off, look a like called *Adijas* or something stupid like that. But I wore them anyway. Why?

Why would I wear something that I know is clearly just a cheap knock-off? Because I wanted the same result that Nike or Adidas provided without having to spend all the money on the shoes. I just wanted to look cool. And it usually worked. At a distance walking by me in the hall, most people would glance down and think I had on name brand shoes. Just don't get close enough to them, otherwise the cover would be blown.

There's a huge difference

I get the privilege to have several people with tons of wisdom pour into my life and faith. One day, I was having a conversation with one of these people, and I was expressing my desire for people to press deeper into a relationship with God. Not to just say that they are a part of the Kingdom, but to live a life that screams it; when you are around them, it's just obvious.

That's when she said to me, "It sounds a lot like the border of Kansas and Colorado. The only thing telling you that you're no longer in Kansas is a sign."

Mind blown.

That pinned down exactly what I was trying to express.

There's a huge difference between being a part of the Kingdom and truly experiencing the Kingdom.

Here's what happens with a lot of us. We say a prayer, make a declaration that Jesus is Lord, and accept God's gift of salvation. We get really excited and leap across the border from the "world" to the Kingdom. Then we stop. That's only as far as we will ever go. We know we need to keep separation from the world and the Kingdom, so we go to church on Sundays, post Instagram photos of Scriptures, and try not to cuss. We put up a border sign so everyone knows we are now in Colorado, not Kansas, even though they look exactly the same. We straddle the border.

We shouldn't want our spiritual lives to only be separated from this world by a border sign. If that's the case, then why even cross the border in the first place? Why not just stay in Kansas? Why go to Colorado if you aren't going to enjoy the beautiful experience of nature? And if you want to go to Colorado and don't want to experience the trees, mountains, streams, lakes, and more then, well, you might be an idiot.

What if I told you there's so much more to the Kingdom and experiencing God in your life than just a border sign? What if I told you if you spent your days pressing closer to God and deeper into the Kingdom, you will experience so much more? Like beautiful mountains and delightful smelling forests and calming lakes.

If we have to put up border signs to distinguish our faith from the world, we need to decide if in our hearts if we actually want to be a part of the Kingdom at all.

———————————

That is the difference between my coffee addiction and taking shortcuts with Halloween or shoes. I think anyone who acknowledges the power of God and claims to want to be a part of it, would agree we need to live our lives differently with Jesus in it. I think we would all agree that we need to spend our days pressing deeper into the Kingdom, not playing patty-cake at the border.

Instead of throwing the paper route bag over our shoulders and calling it a costume, what if our faith was more like my coffee addiction?

I'm *all* in when it comes to coffee. I consume so much coffee that eventually, the coffee started to consume me. My day is shaped around it, I can't function without it, and everyone I know, knows how much coffee is a part of my life.

The truth is, most of us live life straddling the border of Kansas and Colorado because the initial taste of Colorado isn't that appealing. You hear all these great things about faith. You hear about the mountains, the trees and the life, but when you get to the border, it doesn't seem worth it. So, you stay there because you know you should, but besides a border sign, your life doesn't look much different than it did before. You buy generic knock-off shoe brands because you are too cheap to pay for the real thing, which is fine, except you want people to think you have the real thing. So, other than going to church on Sundays and maybe a few other small things, like volunteering a little bit at your church, your life hasn't truly been changed. It doesn't look that much different and that's because you haven't really experienced God's blessings in your life.

Acquired taste

Faith is an acquired taste like coffee. Most people think faith and salvation is this glorious and awesome tasting thing, but the reality is, coffee and faith are acquired tastes. I've talked with a lot of people who say they think coffee tastes burnt or bitter; and they are partially right. It's not usually the initial, immediate taste that draws us in to coffee. It's the culture. It's the subtly of the flavors. It's the hints of cherry notes or subtle nut taste in the coffee. It's the experience and how it helps you.

Faith, like coffee, is not appealing to most at first. To a lot of people faith has a bitter taste—and it does. I'm not trying to commit blasphemy to the power of faith and salvation, but what I'm trying to say is living a life devoted to following Jesus and advancing the Kingdom is not delicious tasting on the surface. You will be asked to sacrifice your life. You will be asked to choose between the future in the Kingdom and your current desires. You will be persecuted. You will be told you're a fool. You will be tricked. You will be taken advantage of. From the initial taste, following Jesus tastes bitter.

It's getting beyond that. It's acquiring the taste, and it's the subtly of the flavors and it's the culture. It's seeing the blessings in your life from following Christ. It's the relationships you build and keep. The community that grows from it and it's about how it changes you. Coffee changes the way you socialize, the way you study for exams, and the way you get prepared for the day in the mornings.

And it's everything like the border of Kansas and Colorado. From the initial taste, Colorado doesn't look that great. In fact, it looks just like Kansas. The only thing distinguishing the two states is some stupid sign. But if you press deeper into Colorado, you will experience something so incredible, so beautiful, and so life-changing you won't ever want to go back. You'll want to invite as many people as possible to experience the beauty you are experiencing.

But you'll never experience that if you stop just past the border, grab a Bible to go Trick or Treating and call yourself a Christian. What's the point of Trick or Treating if I'm just going to be lazy about my costume? Why not just go buy candy and say I went Trick or Treating? What's the point of pretending to have name brand shoes if I'm not willing to pay the price they cost? What's the point of our faith if we aren't going to advance past the border? Why straddle the border and pretend you have something that you don't really have? Just because you are "technically" in Colorado doesn't mean you are white water rafting.

I want a faith in the mountains of Colorado, not just at the border of Colorado and Kansas. Our lives should resemble the Kingdom of God so well we don't need a sign for people to see we are in Colorado. If you're stuck at the border of Kansas and Colorado, set your coordinates west and just drive. Trust me, soon enough you'll get past the initial taste and experience what we're talking about.

Don't live your faith on the border, because let's be honest, compared to the mountains in Colorado, the border is simply lame. And so are Mexican knock-off Adidas shoes.

A TOILET PAPER FAITH

I may not have my doctorate or be a genius, but if there is one thing I know for sure, it is that the toilet paper goes *over* and not *under*. And don't you dare try to debate with me. If you like the toilet paper to go under, not over, then I don't like you, and if I ever use your bathroom, I will switch it. There are many legitimate debates in this world and that is not one of them.

I'm certainly not a conspiracy theorist. I don't believe there are robot zombies secretly being held at Area 51, and I don't believe the president has a secret plot to destroy America, but I do believe my beautiful wife is a part of a conspiracy. Not a conspiracy that involves robot zombies or destroying America, but a conspiracy that involves toilet paper and my sanity.

We've been married for several years now, and my wife knows I'm an *over* guy. I can't stand it when the toilet paper is under. You would think after this many years of marriage, she would learn. I'm pretty confident in saying, I don't think in all our years being married, she has changed the toilet paper roll and put the toilet paper *over* even once.

Every time I go into the bathroom and the toilet paper roll has been changed by her, I have to switch from *under* to *over*. Now, as the logical guy I am, I put the pieces together. Knowing I don't like it *under*, and being married as long as we have been, any respectful person would acknowledge that desire within your spouse and with pure love in your heart, make it a gesture of your undying love to put the toilet paper on the way they prefer.

Nope.

Not my wife.

After countless conversations about the toilet paper; it's efficiency and convenience of being *over* not *under*, she claims she doesn't think or look when she puts the new toilet paper roll on. That it "just so happens" to end up *under* every single time. *Every. Single. Time.* I'm no mathematician, but based on the statistics, the probability of it happening that often is not good. It's a conspiracy, and I'm convinced of it. A conspiracy to intentionally put it *under* to drive me insane. Then when I'm insane, she can have access to all my treasure chests of money. I am rich after all: I chose ministry as a career.

"Because the Bible said so"

I've been apart of churches my entire life. Churches that are very traditional and churches that think they are cool because they open their services with Coldplay or U2 songs. But in all my abundant years in churches, one of the things that baffles me

A Toilet Paper Faith

the most in the "Christian world" is its view on alcohol. I've noticed that there are typically two major base camps for churches and Christians when it comes to this topic.

The first base camp dreads alcohol. They are morally opposed to drinking it, because it's bad. This camp cannot differentiate between the Bibles direct conversations and mandates to not overindulge yourself in alcohol and drinking it normally. What's most bewildering about this first base camp I'm describing is the lack of awareness they portray in this mindset.

I know a guy who hates alcohol. Now not in the way the that is understandable. His father wasn't an alcoholic and abusive, and he wasn't recovering from a twelve-step program. No. He hated alcohol because—and I quote—"It's not a Godly way to live my life." Okay. If we stopped there, that could make sense on some level, and you could probably respect his values as noble. But let's dig a bit deeper. Everyday this guy wakes up in the morning and heads to work. On his way he always stops at the Quik-Shop and gets himself a fifty-two ounce mega-cup of Mountain Dew to get him through the morning. He doesn't really like coffee so the Mountain Dew is his coffee. The Mountain Dew is gone by eleven a.m. At lunch, he and some buddies need to eat fairly quickly, so they head to Wendy's. He grabs a juicy hamburger, fries and a sixteen-ounce cup of Dr. Pepper that he refills twice. When he gets home from work, his wife is tired. She asks him if he'd be okay with a Little Caesars Pizza for dinner. He nods his head apathetically but deep in his soul he is super pumped, because their "Three-Meat Treat Pizza" is his favorite! At the end of the night, him and his wife sit down to watch television, and he grabs a bag of chips from the pantry and snacks until bedtime.

Now I'm not one to lay down assumptions, but I think the evidence is clear. See this is the problem with this first base camp. Should the issue here really be the alcohol? Or maybe, just maybe the issue is this man's poor health. The soda he is consuming is filled with high fructose corn syrup. HFCS is not even sugar. It's a concentrated replacement of sugar so they can a put whole lot less product in the drink for a whole lot less money and still get that sweetness they desire. The flavor in soda is artificial flavoring. Another chemical. Now the verdict is still out on the health statistics of HFCS and artificial flavoring, but I can assure you, drinking that much of a concentrated chemical compound cannot possibly be good for you. I think common sense will finish off the rest of his day for you: the fast food, the pizza and the chips. I think you catch my drift here.

The second base camp, as you can probably already guess, goes the opposite direction. The second category loves alcohol. They want people to know they drink so people will think them and their church is hip and relevant. They use alcohol to make a statement. Since Jesus drank wine, therefore they feel the responsibility to let everyone else know that. And just as the first base camp never drinks it, this category may easily border on over consumption. But you'll often find them saying things like, "I can do it as long as I don't get drunk."

I knew of this one church that was cool. The worship band wore the coolest clothes, the pastor had great charisma, and lots of people went to this church. This church prided itself on being hip and cool. I knew of one of their home-group Bible studies that always had alcohol there. It wasn't casual, but they pretended it was. It was a statement. They offered beer at the Bible study because they wanted people to know that it was okay to drink even at a church sponsored function. They always talked about the different types of beer so people knew that they drink alcohol enough to know the fermentation process. One guy even brewed his own beer! And when they go to Applebee's, why get an iced tea when they can get a beer? This way when someone they know walks in they can see them drinking the beer and think, *Oh wow, that's one of the pastors from my church and he's drinking beer! This church must be cool and non judgmental!*

It's perfect logic, right? Make alcohol a big deal but make it look casual. Then people will think you're a cool Christian.

Walk in the Spirit

If you're going to take a high moralistic stance on alcohol—because it's mentioned in the Bible a few times—then you better dig a bit deeper. It doesn't matter if you're highly "for" alcohol or "against" it; and frankly I don't care. The issue the Bible is laying out in the scriptures has very little to do with the alcohol itself. Scripture communicates to not over indulge in it; hence the word "drunkenness." And it's not even solely about alcohol. It's the overconsumption of *anything*. In Galatians, Paul is writing a letter and he mentions drunkenness. Yes, but he also mentions orgies. Oh and there's also jealousy and anger. If you pay attention, you'll catch what Paul is communicating. It's the very first sentence of that scripture in Galatians 5:16: "But I say, walk by the Spirit, and you will not gratify the desires of the flesh."

All the things listed in the subsequent verses are all things of fleshy desire, such as drunkenness. Our flesh wants to over indulge in alcohol because it feels good when you do it. Also, you may be inclined to run down the street naked which provides entertainment for everyone you're with and potentially the Internet crowd when that video goes viral. Our flesh wants orgies because it feels good. Our flesh wants to indulge in anger and jealousy because we're selfish human beings. Paul is simply calling the people of Galatia out in this letter and basically says, "Stop! This is not what you should be focusing your energy on!"

In Ephesians 5, Paul writes a letter to the Ephesian church and basically says the same thing. He calls them out on their junk. But again, the context of his letter is about living wise lives and to not be foolish.

Scriptures keep calling us back to what's important: *Jesus*. It's important that we continue to or start to walk in spirit and walk wisely. And that's what so disturbing about these extreme stances on alcohol. They're irrelevant. Beer is a drink. Wine is a drink. A martini is a drink. What if we stopped focusing on whether the drink is bad or not and simply not overindulge ourselves on *anything*. Because I will be bold enough here to say that the guy drinking that much soda and eating that much junk and unhealthy foods is overindulging, and it's just as bad as drunkenness on wine.

It's funny to me sometimes as I watch church groups and youth groups and such. They will order loads of greasy pizza and dozens of two-liters of soda and say a prayer that goes like this, "Dear Lord, thank you for this day and bless this food to our bodies." Really!? Bless that chemical compound of high fructose corn syrup and 90 percent fat in that pizza? God's probably laughing like, "Yeah right!"

What I'm saying here is this: drink beer if you think it tastes good, not because of a moral stance that means nothing. If you had a relative die because of alcoholism, and you feel convicted to not drink it, then don't. That is an honorable stance. But just remember, people die all the time because of obesity and the crap they put in their bodies. So maybe some of us should have those same convictions about food.

It's not about the alcohol itself. It's about the motive to use it. I like white wine because it tastes good. I will not drink red wine, though. Not because it's bad, but because it gives me heartburn. See the difference?

Policy, policy, policy!

Let me tell you about my initial entry into the vocational local church ministry. I was all about my toilet paper preferences. I loved my policies, procedures, and rules. I wasn't loving people well. Advancing the Kingdom was my motive, but not my result. I spent my days crafting my ministries around the toilet paper being *over* not *under*. I argued with people, criticized people, and spent my days crafting policies so people in my ministry would understand the importance of hypothetically always putting the toilet paper *over*. They needed to understand why my way was the best. And if they didn't like it, then they could leave. I did it all in the name of ministry and in the name of Jesus.

Now there is some validity to policies and procedures, because realistically the toilet paper needs to be hung and be accessible. So policies aren't aren't all bad, it just became my main focus and my main focus needed to be loving people like Jesus.

The truth was, I needed to love better. As a Christ follower, and more specifically as a pastor, I have two main jobs: grow closer to God every day and love people well. Love people like Jesus so the Kingdom can be advanced.

What if we all did that instead of complaining about music preferences in church, judging church leadership for everything they say and do, and carrying offenses about everything the church does? What if the church wasn't for us to debate about which direction the toilet paper needs to go, but for those who need to hear about Jesus? What if we didn't spend our time debating whether alcohol is good or bad, or whether gay people should be invited to the potluck dinner and just love like Jesus?

I'm a policy guy, trust me. I love contracts, addendums, calendars, meetings, and itineraries. I love them all, I just do! But sometimes, in those moments, I realize how insignificant those things are to the end goal.

People who are not separating themselves from the world get caught up in things in the world that don't matter. My wife and I would both agree toilet paper accomplishes the same thing and how you should use it (don't get me started on whether you fold or crumble your toilet paper!) regardless of whether it's *over* or *under*. So why do we spend all our energy arguing over something that doesn't matter when the result and application is supposed to be the same? Shouldn't we be focusing our energy on more important things?

Just wipe already!

So what is the take-away from this, then?

We all need to spend our days pressing deeper into the Kingdom and not spend all our energy on things that don't matter; like the policies of our personal ministry here on earth. Things like should I drink alcohol? Swearing is bad. Which R-rated movie is not a sin to go see? Should I eliminate Santa from Christmas? You know, all the stuff that in the long run, doesn't matter as much as we probably think they do.

Most of the things I'm talking about matter on some level. Please don't hear me wrong. I'm simply saying that they don't matter more than loving people like Jesus.

Listen, you like hymns? Cool. There's a community that will do that for you. The pastor's sermons too long? I'm sure there's a church with shorter sermons. Church too big for you? There's a smaller one down the street—probably singing hymns. Ha! Don't like the urinal cakes in the men's restroom? I'm sure there a cooler church with fancier urinal cakes for you to pee on. This is what I mean. These are all insignificant preferences.

I think it's time we stop debating whether we should drink alcohol while we pray for God to bless the pizza, chips, and soda to our bodies. Maybe we should worry about more important things like cherishing the bodies of which God has asked us to be good stewards.

I've noticed as I've read through the scriptures over the years that this is a constant theme. I only used alcohol as an example because I was drinking wine as I was writing this and need justification. But seriously, if you look through the scriptures its so common. All of Paul's letters, all of Jesus' teachings usually center around this idea of "Stop focusing on the stuff that doesn't matter and just pursue God."

We all love Jesus, need Jesus and need to love *like* Jesus. That's the end result. Just like my wife and I both need toilet paper. At the end of the day it really makes no difference whether it's *over* or *under*. We both need it and use it. Why talk about what doesn't matter?

CONGESTED WORSHIP

I've always contemplated becoming a doctor, but it's not about helping others. In fact, it's a purely selfish motive. I want to become a doctor so I can research, test, and develop a way to take my nose, lungs, all my sinus and asthma-related parts, and replace them with less awful ones. I am always congested. To be honest, I'm not even sure if I've ever breathed normally in my life. In the year 2006, I was seventeen years old, and I actually had surgery on my sinuses to help relieve pressure. My doctor told me it was like I had a sinus infection for seventeen years. I believed him because his ethnicity was Indian, and most Indian people tend to be really smart.

On top of my ridiculous sinus issues, I have really sensitive asthma, and the two of them don't blend well. It's a smoothie no one wants to drink. So when normal people get colds, I get bronchitis or pneumonia. It's always a delightful time. This period each year of about two to three weeks usually involves me eating saltines; drinking Gatorade; binge watching *Boy Meets World*, *Friends*, or *The Office*; and not showering for days on end. Now that I'm married, I can also get my wife to do things for me, so I don't have to get off the couch.

When our daughter, Aubrie, was only two or three months old, she got her first cold. I can't help, but assume I contributed some of my awesome genetics for that. It was really hard for me as a new dad to watch my daughter struggle with congestion. Now that my daughter is older, that struggle hasn't gotten easier. When we check on her at night and can see her struggle to breath normally, it breaks our hearts. And honestly, it scares us a bit. What is so difficult for me, is I know how she is when she's not congested. She's fun, cheerful, laughing, and nowadays, waits until I turn around and then with delight, will dump the dogs food into his water bowl, and then follow that with dumping his water bowl all over the floor. She's enjoying life, by breathing normally in its purest form, and it's a joy to watch—except for the dog food. I hate that.

Scraping the barrel

In usual fashion on Saturday nights, I don't sleep well. I spend my nights contemplating the worship services I have to lead the next day. I think about which team member will be late to rehearsal, how many of our greeters won't show up, whether my voice will be pitchy, and whether the band will play a tight set. You know, the things that don't matter, but you spend your time dwelling on anyway.

Well on this particular Saturday night, my daughter was

struggling with congestion. She had a really hard time falling asleep, because she was so uncomfortable. After a while my smokin' hot wife finally got her to fall asleep. My wife and I checked on her probably a hundred times that night to make sure she could still breathe at all.

After creepily staring into my daughters crib for a long time, just admiring God's amazing creation, I made my way to our bedroom to get ready for bed. And we can be honest here. We all have done it. You go in to check on your child sleeping and find yourself, with your head tilted slightly to the left looking down upon your child, grinning like a sociopath. It's creepy and you know it. But somehow it's socially acceptable to do to your own children. If you don't believe me that it's creepy, try it with a friend or significant other tonight. When they freak out—and they will—tell them you were just admiring God's creation. I bet they don't find it endearing.

As I lay in bed that night, thinking about the things that don't matter for our church services, God prompted my heart with the overwhelming thought of congestion. He kept telling me my voice may sound good the next morning because I wasn't having any sinus issues, but it didn't hide the fact my spiritual life was very congested.

That week in particular, and the few weeks prior, my faith was on a spiritual Tilt-A-Whirl. If you've been a Christian for any amount of time, you can relate. As a pastor, there's a pressure to perform and to have it all together. In fact when you do something a little wrong, people want to call in the mob and make sure you know you screwed up.

My job—week in and week out—is to usher people into

the presence of the Lord and host the Holy Spirit. Yup, that's no pressure at all. Get up in front of my congregation every week and try to pull off a killer worship music set and to make sure it's authentic. And if there's a week you are just a little off, people want to start the next national worship leader search to replace you.

When you have to do this every week, on top of life happening to you, it's just not the same fiery dynamic every week. Some weeks, I hear the Lord speak and guide me with clarity. Those weeks are awesome, because my job becomes easy. I sit back and enjoy the ride. It's like God is shouting the songs the people need to sing and is simultaneously running the soundboard, the computer slides, leading the music, and preaching at the same time. It is always awesome on those weeks.

And other weeks—in full transparency—the last thing I want to do is sing songs to Jesus. Some Sundays, I just want to sleep in and watch *House Hunters* all day. This story was one of those weeks. I was emotionally exhausted, and the last thing I wanted to do was go into church the next morning and be a pastor. On these weeks, I'm scraping the bottom of my worship barrel trying to scrape together any bit of authenticity I have.

Surprise, surprise!

I can still remember when my daughter was born. Since she was our first born, there was nine full months of preparation and "pinning" of Pinterest things. And honestly, I didn't realize the amount of preparation that went into it. I thought my part was done; my enjoyable part of impregnating my wife. But as it turns out, that is not the case. Men! Listen to me! You may think it's fun to get your wife pregnant, but remember this advice. If you do . . . a box will appear at your doorstep a month or two later, and like me, you will be disappointed when you find out it is not full of party supplies to celebrate your manhood. Nope.

It will be a very heavy box that is filled with four hundred and twenty-seven pieces of different sized wood pallets and a bag of sixty-eight multi-sized screws. The instructions will literally be five pictures, two of them showing you how to remove the wood from the box and what a screw is in case your didn't already know. *This is our reward. This is our prize.* To figure out how to take all those pieces and turn it into a crib or dresser or whatever the heck it is, with only five pictures. Thanks a lot, IKEA!

The planning and preparation process for the arrival of our daughter was madness. I felt like everyday we were getting more and more packages in the mail. And just when you begin to feel weary of the process, you open a package to find a tiny, little pink ballerina outfit that makes your heart melt. Well played, mother in-law. Well played.

There were baby shower preparations, furniture building, clothing acquisitions, and room painting to do. Also men, think logically about this. Can your pregnant wife be in a small bedroom with paint fumes? Exactly. You will be doing that one alone with a hormonal pregnant woman telling you the spots you missed. This is another prize at the bottom of the Cracker Jack box for you.

The point here is that we prepared a lot for this baby. The anticipation for our daughter to arrive created an exciting stirring in our hearts and in those closest to us. There were parties, gifts, and lots of smiles. In fact, we were so prepared we even scheduled an induction for the baby. Well, the doctors did because of some health issues. But that allowed both sets of our parents, who all live eleven-hundred miles away to plan a trip out in time for the birth. Everything was lined up perfectly, the room was ready, we had enough diapers, food, clothes, toys, furniture, and even had a date we were going to bring this baby into this world.

———————

On the weekend before Ashley's Monday induction date, all the family was scheduled to arrive. They would all arrive on Friday and Saturday, come to church with us, and be ready to welcome little Aubrie to the world on Monday. My mom, step-dad, and little sister arrived on Friday evening, and we got them settled in. On Saturday, I had a leadership meeting at the church in the morning, and then we were going to meet up with my in-laws on Saturday afternoon. That's when it happened.

While I was at the meeting, Ashley and my mom were home in the kitchen eating a late breakfast and chatting away. Amidst their conversation, Ashley interrupted, "Oh man. Yea, okay. Um. I'm wet. Very wet." She stood up embarrassed but excited realizing that it was her water that broke, not a sudden loss of bladder control. After confirming what was happening, they reached out to call me.

One of things I learned about being respectful is while in a meeting with others, you do not answer your phone if it rings. What they didn't tell me, was that rule doesn't apply when your wife was nine months pregnant. Well I felt my phone vibrating in my pocket, I glanced at it, and saw it was my wife. I ignored it. Twenty seconds later, she called again. Now if I'm busy in my office at work and my wife calls two times in a row, I know to answer it immediately. But this time, to be respectful for the meeting I was in, I ignored it again. About a minute later, I get a missed call from my mom and my little sister.

Obviously I'm not telling this story to boast about my common sense. Any sane person would think, *This many calls in a row, and my wife is nine months pregnant, I better check to make sure things are okay.* Not me. What I think instead is, *Come on guys. What's their problem? Ashley knows that I don't answer my phone in meetings, and she knows I'm at this meeting. So disrespectful. They probably wants me to pick up lunch meat or something stupid.*

About another minute or two goes by and across the room, I see our previous youth pastor's phone light up. He looks at it perplexingly and ignores it as well. It was my wife, too. Then another lady in our meeting had just left the meeting a little early, but comes back in the meeting gladly interrupting and says to me while handing me her phone, "Um . . . you need to answer your phone because you're having a baby." With wide eyes and freaked out like the ten-year-old version of me after watching the movie *Child's Play*, I answered the phone. After yelling at me, I was told to come home immediately, because that baby was coming now.

I hung up the phone and my lead pastor urgently shouted at me to hurry home and the others in the room followed his lead of shouting. Not knowing what to do and still in shock, I began to ramble and try to explain why I didn't answer my phone to everyone in the room. In a somewhat laughing tone I said, "I was just thinking how Ashley knows I don't answer my phone in meetings and she kept calling. And I started thinking . . ." and before I could finish, my lead pastor shouted again, "Shut up and go home!" I grabbed my things, hopped in my car, blasted some heavy metal music and head banged my way home with excitement.

And, while at the time, it was a total shock to us, knowing my daughter's personality now at two years old, it doesn't surprise me even a little that she came early. My daughter is the most strong-willed, persistent child . . . and I have no clue where she got that from.

Are you ready?

That's the funny thing about babies. You can plan for them all you want, but sometimes, they just come whenever they want, and you have to be ready. Aubrie was not just two days early for her induction date, the induction date was actually four days early from her due date. So it was really a surprise when she came before the induction date. She was six days early total. That's why you have to be prepared and just enjoy the anticipation with expectancy.

We had done all the preparations we could and just had to wait. We couldn't really make the baby come whenever we wanted. But because we were prepared for our little angel, when she did decide to come, even six days early, we were not only ready, but we were prepared to embrace her arrival with joy and laughter.

In the months leading up to my daughters birth, I read countless articles and had endless conversations with people telling me how amazing it is to have a child. To be apart of the birthing process, to experience the arrival. It wasn't that I didn't believe them, because I did; but it was just that I didn't have a frame of reference since it was my first child.

Then she was born.

I have never experienced such joy, adoration, amazement, beauty, and mesmerizing awe—all at once. It's almost unfathomable and unexplainable how much I instantaneously loved her when I first saw her. She was mine to love with all my heart. Nothing else mattered. I didn't care if I had a tough week at work. I didn't care how many people didn't like me at the church. I didn't care about our debt. I didn't care about the bills that were due. Not only that, it didn't matter all the mistakes I made in my life, how insecure I was, how much I didn't like myself or my body and more. None of that mattered. All that mattered was my daughter was here, and I got to embrace her with all my love. I got to brag about her to everyone. And most importantly, get ready for the incredible and painful ways she would change my life.

Then it dawned on me: *this is the kind of expectancy we should have with the Lord and the way we worship on Sunday mornings at church.*

Distracted again

There are way too many hipster "lead worshippers" out there. Some of whom who have probably written worship songs about how much they love TOMS Shoes and plaid shirts. And with all of these different worship leaders, comes many different philosophies on worship and what it means to worship in church on a Sunday morning. Hopefully though, we can all agree that TOMS Shoes are the most uncomfortable pair of shoes that has ever existed, and if wearing them makes me cool, then I choose to be lame.

But let's all be honest here. Even if you aren't a worship leader, we all think we know everything there is to know about worship and how to worship. We may pretend with a false humility we don't, but really, we all do. I know I do. I hate it when someone questions the way I do things and my philosophies on worship. Like right now for example. I am literally writing a chapter on a philosophy of worship and I truly think I'm right. So if you disagree with this chapter, you should probably go read your Bible some more and get your life right with Christ. Because if you disagree with me, then you are clearly living in sin.

But through my observations, I feel like there is something that has happened to our worship on Sunday mornings. Our congregations are distracted. Something that should be fresh, sacred, and willing to move with the Holy Spirit has turned into the most predictable series of events out there.

What is lacking here is expectancy—on the Lord. Churches and congregations have *expectations*, not *expectancy*. We all have these expectations. Whether we admit them or not, we expect things to go a certain way; in fact, we demand it.

We show up on Sundays, usually a little late, and proceed to scuffle to find a parking spot. After walking a mile from the parking lot to the door, we make our way to the children's area to check-in our children to the children's programming. And it better be good or we'll leave and go somewhere that has a better, more fun program for our children. After that, we make our way to the auditorium and sit in the same area we do every week. We hope they sing songs we know, we look around at the cool lights and stage decorations, and hope the pastor's sermon is interesting and under thirty minutes.

There is a lack of expectancy because we've focused too much in on our expectations. There is certainly no lack of preparation on the church's side. But the congregations expectations put a weight on the church staff, where in turn, the preparation is designed for execution, not the arrival of the Holy Spirit.

Making a flame

Imagine a fireplace. I like to think of our corporate worship on Sunday mornings as a fireplace. And I like to relate Sunday morning worship services *with* expectancy as a fireplace with really dry wood in it. You prepare the fireplace, assemble the dry wood, you assemble the wood strategically to make sure air flow can move around, and you have all the tools and accessories needed for the fire. All that fireplace needs at this point is a little spark to catch fire. That wood is ready to burn hard and fast, it just awaits the spark.

What tends to happen is that we fill our fireplaces with damp wood: wood that is clearly not prepared to be burned. This wood can still catch fire, but you have use many, many different sparks and even then, a fire isn't guaranteed. So at the risk there might not be a fire, we use all the resources we can think of. We use lighter fluid, paper, kindling—anything possible to make that fire happen.

When we don't have expectancy, we try to make our own fire, a fire the Holy Spirit should be making. We use any resource we can as lighter fluid and kindling instead of coming with expectancy and waiting on the Lord which is being dry wood.

And I'm not saying lighter fluid is bad. But imagine if you add that to dry wood. That flame will burn your eyebrows off! It's using the resources to enhance the fire from the Holy Spirit not to create fire. He doesn't need it!

————————

It makes me wonder how many of us come to church on a consistent basis as damp wood. It's not that we can't catch flame and be a part of the fire. The element missing here is expectancy.

What if we walked in the doors on Sunday mornings and didn't need lighter fluid? One spark of the Holy Spirit and we could burn purely without lighter fluid.

We need to plan and prepare. That's the whole point here. Expectancy isn't the art of doing nothing and waiting for something to happen. It's the art of preparation and anticipation. We're not planning to manufacture, which can be a misconception. We need to be ready, dry wood, as we await the arrival of the Holy Spirit.

Just like the expectancy we had for our daughter, we need to have that same kind of anticipation for the Lord's Spirit to move us. We were so excited for her arrival, that we planned. We decorated, painted, talked about it to everyone, more than I can even remember. Her arrival was unpredictable, we just had to be ready. We didn't do those things to manufacture her arrival; it was done *for* her arrival.

When you live with expectancy daily, you need to plan. You need to do what you need to do for the Spirit's arrival. That's one of the mindsets for Sunday mornings. We plan and prepare, allowing the Holy Spirit to move in big ways. And when He does, we are ready!

Planning and preparing looks different to each person. I could sit here and list for you a million and one ways to plan and prepare. But would it be authentic? I think that's the search. That's the pursuit. How one person prepares and plans is going to be different from the person next to them. I would say though, a great place to start would be to spend time in scripture and ask God to speak to your heart about it. Be creative and innovative!

I think it's important to live everyday with such anticipation, expectation, and non-congested clarity because you can plan all you want for the arrival, and should; but the Holy Spirit can move at any point, in anyone. When we do this and the Holy Spirit moves, we can embrace it fully prepared and ready to get our worlds rocked.

GUILTY LATTE

Let me be frank with you, and no, I'm not changing my name. One of my biggest flaws in my ministry or even my life is dealing with charity.

Don't interrupt my latte

A few years ago, I was at Starbucks with a friend in Phoenix. We ended up on the subject of charity in regards to the Christian faith. We decided that in Christianity, we talk a lot about what it means to live out our faith on a day-to-day basis, yet a lot of us don't actually do it. Honestly, it's like the women who spend hours on Pinterest "pinning" creative ideas for the home, recipes, and hair bows yet seldom have the motivation to actually use them. In return this creates a psychological dilemma in which these women actually think they are creative because they spend hours a day on an electronic device thinking about creativity. It's also very similar to when I have an elaborate plan to workout at the gym and eat healthy then a week later I see a Chipotle and decide I like burritos better. But as soon as I'm done eating that delicious burrito, I'll be sure to complain to you about how frustrated I am I'm not losing weight.

Of course, with my impenetrable luck, a lady came into the Starbucks holding a cardboard sign. I watched this lady as she made her way to a table in the store and without success moving onto the next. I figured she was going to mention how hungry she was. Then I remembered I didn't have any cash. I was totally saved once again with the fact that I was poor too (except for the $4.75 latte I was consuming).

She finally drug her pathetic self over to my table and held up her cardboard sign. Finally getting a good look at the board, I saw it had pictures of her two children on it. In the other hand was a piece of paper. She started speaking what was clearly a rehearsed speech, and I interrupted her. I told her I didn't have any cash. She proceeded to shake her head and explain to me it wasn't money she wanted. She waved the piece of paper in my face and was clearly frustrated from the prior rejections from other tables.

I took the paper from her and saw it was an electric bill. I looked at her confused, and she began to tell me how she lost her job and needed to pay her electric bill for the safety of her children. I should also mention that not only did this take place in Phoenix, but the average temperature was above one hundred degrees. To not have air conditioning in Phoenix is like going to Starbucks and getting a Frappuccino. It's just stupid. Frappuccinos are *not* coffee. Go to Dairy Queen if you want a milk shake.

Anyway, I suddenly realized my excuse of not having cash was suddenly invalid and this lady really did have a need for air conditioning. I began to examine the bill when I noticed something interesting. Her electric bill was two-hundred and sixty seven dollars and none of that was from late fees. Somehow this lady racked up a massive electric bill and wanted me to pay for it. That large of an electric bill, even in Phoenix it is quite the accomplishment. Now using my detective skills, I knew if this lady was truly in desperate need, chances were good that she didn't have a large home that would justify a bill that large.

Immediately my skepticism went through the roof. I knew I couldn't pay for this electric bill because 1) I couldn't financially pull something like that off and 2) well, I didn't want to. But I did brew up a good excuse.

At that time I was working on staff at a church that had a campus literally minutes down the road. The church was large and had a ministry with great resources to handle situations similar to this ladies'. I told her I could not help her, but then explained to her that this church down the street may be able to help.

She immediately said no and said she would not go to a church. I sent my condolences and sent her on her way. Rolling my eyes and shaking my head in annoyance, I sipped my latte and I continued our conversation on living the Christian life well.

Skepticism seems to be a giant hurdle for me every time I

attempt to extend my love in the form of charity. Of course I felt guilty after my encounter with that lady in Starbucks. I think the source of my guilt was mixed feelings of skepticism and awkwardness. For starters, I didn't believe her story. It seemed like an act to smooth talk someone into paying for her ridiculously high electric bill. And I also didn't know how to handle the situation.

What I wanted to do was stand up, grab her by her shoulders, and shake her. And I wanted to yell at her. Yell at her for being a mooch, a liar, and for being selfish. I wanted to tell her to stop wasting our time and to spend her time looking for a job instead of pan handling. I want to help people out, but I want the discernment to be able to know when they are taking me for a ride. Unfortunately, I lack that skill and instead of discernment, I settle for judgment.

Beggars are so annoying

At the church I currently have the privilege of working at, we were finishing up a mini-remodel to our auditorium when this next story happened. After a grueling two weeks of seventy to eighty hours per week, we were finally on our last day and the finish line was near. To say I was tired is an understatement. Our last project of the day was putting the finishing touches on our new light rack in the auditorium. Our two youth pastors at the time were on the scissor lift installing some lights while I was on the ground getting the screws, nuts, and washers assembled for them. I was mainly on the ground because of my fear of heights. Unfortunately for this situation, my fear of heights backfired and thrust me into this story.

No one else was in the building but the three of us as we carried on with delirious laughter and jokes. It was then, in the midst of my highest level of exhaustion that it happened. I heard someone say from a distance, "Hello?" I turned around to see who it was, and I didn't recognize them. And of course, with my being a professional skeptic, I knew it was a lady going to ask for money, and I certainly didn't want to deal with them.

I looked up to the scissor lift with disgust on my face and graciously, our main youth pastor at the time responded to the woman's greeting and introduced himself from twenty-two feet in the air while I blatantly ignored her. Unfortunately, when she was done feeding us her bold-faced lie of a story, he tossed the responsibility over to me. With an irritable sigh, I made my way toward her. With a quick, disingenuous "Hi," I greeted the woman and made my way to the main church office. I didn't speak a word to her as I picked up the phone to call the woman in charge of our benevolence fund. Meanwhile, this needy lady, who was accompanied by a man, began to tell me her sob story.

I didn't believe her story for a second. She told me she met the man that brought her from the motel where she was staying. I did believe that part of the story because she was wearing a shirt that didn't come below her midriff and her jeans were riding so low on her hips I could see things I didn't want to see. It certainly looked like she came from a motel.

Yes, I am aware I am a horrible person for thinking those thoughts; but I digress.

Regardless of the clothing she wore, or the lack there of, she was clearly tripping on some kind of illegal substance. Her eyes were blood shot, she was jittery, talked a mile a minute, not to mention she sounded winded from a normal conversation.

I dialed our Care Ministry director with the most irritated look on my face. When I reached the ministry director, I handed the phone over and let this lady tell her sob story to the person in charge. When she was done, of course, the man who was accompanying her requested to speak on the phone as well. I rolled my eyes, handed him the phone and mumbled to myself, "When it rains it pours, apparently."

When they were done begging, I got back on the phone, and the ministry director told me to give them some pre-loaded cards to the local grocery store/gas station. She then asked me to pray for them. Now, let me explain something here. The Care Ministry director *always* prays for people that she talks with. Whether it's in person or on the phone, she always tells them about Jesus and prays for them. Now why in the world would she ask me to pray for them? Divine intervention I'm convinced. I believe God knew my heart was hardened to the situation, and He forced me to be verbally compassionate. Either that or God just needed a laugh and figured I would be a perfect candidate for such a situation.

———————————

It was just a few days later and we were in a staff meeting. In the middle of our meeting, we get interrupted by a man. I turn around to see who it was, and of course, as luck would have it, it was the same man from a few days before who accompanied the woman. The man was shy and very quiet. He gave us the same story from a few days prior. He claimed he was hungry;

that he and his boy were really hungry and hadn't eaten any-thing since the food they were able to get with the food card we gave them just a few days prior.

I turned back around and rolled my eyes. *The guy comes back in again just a few days later? Come on now, there are over one hundred churches in town, go bother another one.* These all were things going through my head in that moment. Our lead pastor in his normal gracious, generous, and genuine nature stepped out in the hallway to address the man. I heard him explain we have a policy to only help someone once a year in order to make our limited resources go as far as possible and to be able to help as many people as we can. You can hear the man ask, "You really get that many requests for help?" to which our lead pastor responds, "All the time, I'm afraid."

You can hear the man continue to plead his case and beg-ging for us to make an exception due to his hunger. Finally breaking down, our lead pastor invites the man to go with him to see if there is anything in our church kitchen's refrigerator. The man began crying, I think, and thanking him. About one minute later, our lead pastor returns to the office and addresses our youth pastor, "Hey, there are like six frozen pizzas in the freezer you use for youth group . . . " and before he could finish, our youth pastor told him to let the man have them all.

When our lead pastor was finished helping the man, he returned to the office with a surprised look on his face. He said, "You'll never guess what just happened." We all looked at him awaiting his story. He began to tell us how he excitedly opened the refrigerator and offered all the frozen pizzas to the man. To which the man replied, "I really appreciate this. But since you said you get a lot of requests, I think I'll take just two pizzas, just in case anyone else comes in and needs some food."

There I was, doing the opposite of exemplifying the love of Christ, and this man seemed to prove the legitimacy of his story as well as exemplify Christ better than I did—and I'm a pastor. That situation literally made me sick to my stomach. I couldn't believe my heart towards this man. God put him in my path twice to love on him, and I failed miserably, simply because I let my skepticism get the best of me.

A skeptical heart

What is it about skepticism that can turn even the biggest Jesus lover into a babbling barbarian? When you read my thoughts and my conversations in these situations, it's clear that my intelligence and logic is no better than a selfish caveman's. In case you're wondering, I know a lot about cavemen. I know they babble and are selfish. I've seen all the Geico commercials, so I know.

Skepticism skews our logic and most importantly our faith. I don't think any of us intend to be skeptics. In fact, I hate that part about myself. But in this world, we are taught we can never be too careful. There's always someone that's going to take advantage, and when I see those people, it causes my anger to trigger and I don't see people like Jesus does.

I think what's admiring about Jesus' character is He didn't see through a skeptic's lens. He sees people the way His father created them—and that's beautiful. There's a story in the Bible where this man was pretty sketchy. He was a tax collector and took people's money—took more than he should have and pocketed the rest. It's kind of like your Internet company. When they charge you eighty dollars for airwaves, you know you're getting ripped off. This guy's name from the Bible was Zacchaeus, but I call him Zachy. Instead of rolling His eyes at Zachy, Jesus invited himself to Zachy's home and engaged in life with this man. He didn't just approach this man, He hung out with this man, went to his house, and probably ate his food.

I think I feel most convicted because Jesus turned the tables. What if I approached charity with the same zeal? When I know someone is taking me for a ride, what if I embraced life with them and showed them, that despite their sin, I love them anyway. Or even better, I don't see them as a sinner but as the beautiful person God created. And hopefully through that love, they will see Jesus.

THE TEMPLE

MARKETPLACE

I am a sucker for homeless people. I've gotten myself to the point to where I will purposely not carry cash when I am in a large city because I know I will give it all away. If I'm honest with myself, I really feel like I care about the poor and have sympathy for them. I mean, within a day, I could be that homeless person. I guess it makes me feel good knowing the money I gave them could be enough to get a meal. I never buy them meals though, because I'm too busy. When I see a homeless person, I usually have a place to be, so taking them to buy a meal would be pretty annoying and out of my way. I mean, I gave them money for food, the least they could do is walk themselves to a Burger

King. I shouldn't have to hold their hand. Plus homeless people are usually weird and talk to themselves. I give them money and the "Big Guy" upstairs gives me a nice big check mark in the charity category. That's how this exchange works.

One evening, I was walking downtown in a major city with my wife when I saw a homeless man on the corner, and I knew I was going to cave. I had ten bucks cash I brought specifically for us to go to a popular cafe, and now I was going to buckle under the pressure and give him my money. I put my head down hoping that would help shield me from making eye contact. When we approached him though, my eye was stolen by what was on the sign he was holding up. "Let's be honest, I'm just going to buy alcohol." I was floored by this man's honesty. Why in the world would he put that on his sign and risk getting rejected? It really baffled me. So, in all my maturity, I approached the man and told him I respected his honesty, gave him my ten bucks and asked what we was going to drink. He said gin.

True charity

I was at a conference, and the speaker was talking about charity. The speaker suggested going to a drive-through sometime and pay for the people behind you. You wouldn't know the people, see the people, etc. It would be a random act of kindness, and then you would drive off with no satisfaction of seeing their reactions. He said it would be "true charity" because we lose the novelty of seeing the people happy which is what makes us feel good. Honestly, I laughed. Why would I do that? Chances are if I'm at the McDonald's drive through, that's because I only have enough money for the Dollar Menu.

Some time after that conference, I was at a Starbucks drive-through, and I decided I would give this true charity thing a shot. And because it was Starbucks, I would only have to buy a drink which would be cheaper than a meal at Wendy's. I thought it was brilliant. This way, if I didn't like this true charity, I wouldn't have to waste a lot of money to figure it out. Just one drink.

I ordered my drink and then told the hippie looking dude behind the window I would like to pay for the vehicle behind me. He looked confused, as if he lost the pot he had stashed in the glove compartment of his car. "Are you sure?" he asked. I didn't think it was a tough request, but I figured he probably smoked a lot of pot. I gave him an eyebrow raise and slowly nodded my head. "Okay man, whatever you say", he replied with a sarcastic tone.

I should have used my rear-view mirror to scope out the vehicle first. Lesson learned. The barista wasn't high, he probably just thought I was stupid. I got my receipt back and the charge was for thirty-six dollars! I thought he made a mistake, because he was a pot smoker. But then I looked in the mirror and I saw a van. I had just purchased coffee and snacks for a van full of teenagers, and they were thrilled. Maybe next time I'll spend less time determining if the barista smokes pot and execute better due diligence.

Now I feel good

During a dinner party with some family friends, the topic of homeless people and charity came up. I shared with them how I felt about charity at that point in my life. I told them it didn't matter what the homeless did with my money once I gave it to them. And as long as I buy coffee for a stranger that counts as charity. Our friends challenged my philosophy. They told me I didn't care about homeless people and, in fact, I could possibly have enabled a habit. Maybe I give a homeless man some money, then he uses it to buy drugs and then overdoses on those drugs. That made me feel really bad. It's true though. My heart was in the wrong place, and I was only giving to charity because I had my own self worth issues, and in a sick, twisted way it helped me feel good about myself. My heart was only buying Starbucks for the car behind me because it was going to fulfill some sort of religious check list.

It reminded me of an old friend I had in junior high and high school. His name was John-Mark. I always thought it was weird that he had two first names. I guess it's biblical. He was the kindest kid you could possibly know and was very talented at a lot of things. Above all of his marvels, running was his specialty. He could run a mile in like two minutes. It was incredible. I loved my times with him, because I learned so much. Fishing was one of those things I didn't know how to do until he showed me. We would go out on the lake with kayaks and just talk while we fished.

There is a very popular saying from an unknown author that says "Give a man a fish; you have fed him for today. Teach a man to fish; and you have fed him for a lifetime." If no one gives anything ever to the homeless, they can starve, but you don't want to spoon feed them either.

This quote sets up the meaning of charity well. When it comes to charity, there tends to be this constant battle between helping out those in real need and those who just feel they are entitled to it.

When you break down this quote, the emphasis is centered around this idea of not spoon feeding the needy. What the quote indirectly implies is a relationship that has value. It says to teach a man to fish. I have only fished a few times since those days in my life, mainly because I think worms are gross, but if I had to rely on fishing for food I could do it. When my friend John-Mark taught me to fish, he would take me out, spend the time with me, make sure I could cast the pole, and put on the bait. There was a relationship. John-Mark took the time to invest in me.

I tell you all this because I think the Starbucks story and this issue on charity are good examples of how we need to check our hearts. Let me stop you before you all run out and schedule appointments with your doctors. I don't mean to medically get your hearts checked. Well, I mean we should all meet with a doctor about it at some point. Good preventive care is always helpful. But what I mean by checking our hearts is we need to observe our motives for what we do. Why do you do what you do?

The concept is the same for our faith. We have to constantly check our hearts to make sure we aren't falling into religious practices for the sake of religion, but we do those things because our hearts are fully in them.

When I examined my heart, I found out deep in my soul I really didn't care for the homeless people. I didn't have a burning passion to help them. I did it because I felt like I had to, and I did it to boost my ego—to make myself feel good.

It was then, at that dinner party, it all came full circle for me. A major Holy Spirit conviction. I did not have a good heart attitude toward charity and the needy. In fact, I had a corrupted one. I was so blind to what true charity was, I caused more harm than good.

Destructive charity

The deception with charity is this: "As long as I give." It doesn't matter the motive, because I gave, and that counts for something. The truth is, if I just give to give, it can actually be more destructive than not giving anything at all. If I just give a man money on the street corner, he may become dependent on my money, and when I stop giving him money, he starves, because all he knows how to do is stand there with his hands out. Or even worse, he could use the money to buy drugs and overdose.

Giving money away is easy. There's no effort involved. I simply determine how much I have, how much I want to give and, in a matter of seconds, I'm on my way. If I were to apply the implications of that popular quote, I would recognize it has nothing to do with the money and everything to do with the relationship. What I could do is take the guy out for lunch and get to know him. Try to help him become a better person and help him grow. Maybe share my faith with him. Like I said earlier, too often it's annoying to take a homeless person to lunch because I would actually have to invest in their lives.

I'm not saying that giving cash to homeless people is wrong. The point is it can be destructive. I may not be thinking about how destructive it could be to just give cash to this homeless man without any relational connection. Not every homeless man will overdose on drugs from the cash I give him, but it's the effect it has on that man by not investing in him. Investing in a relationship with a homeless man is the best way to keep your heart in the right place.

The extremist

Charity and I don't mesh well together. It's probably because I'm an extremist. I either feel really bad for them and give them all of my money or I'm a huge skeptic who thinks everything they say is a big, fat lie. There's no middle ground for me.

I think what's hard for me is being a pastor and balancing this charity thing. There are a lot of days when I'm in the office by myself and, with my infinite luck, those seem to be the days when people come in begging for money. I'm ashamed to admit this, but some days I just don't have the energy to deal with them, so I lock the front door. Now before you condemn me for being a terrible person, realize that God and I are already hashing through my terribleness and trying to fix it. I really think the deciding factor for my generosity is if I see them on the street looking homeless as opposed to coming to the church asking for gas money. It's a really good measuring stick. I know, it's brilliant. Not!

But as I sit in my office, and I hear them enter the building, my heart sinks. Generally because most of the people don't attend our church and just want our money. In my humanness, I automatically decide within five seconds whether they are really poor or a really poor liar. And again, hashing through my terribleness, I usually decide their fate by how many teeth they have or if they smell like cigarette smoke. Subconsciously I think,

If they can afford to buy cigarettes, they don't need gas money.

The good thing for me is we have a Care Ministry at our church. So I take their information and call the ministry lead. She will then call that person and assess the situation. But I observed this ministry lead one day handle someone asking for money and it blew my mind.

This gal pops in my office and begins to give me this long story about how she has no money, has a ton of kids, and needs to get to a city an hour away for cancer testing. Her car was supposedly on empty, and she was in desperate need of gas money. As I listen, I see she's missing several teeth and reeks of cigarette smoke. She was certainly overweight, bordering on obese, so I wondered how she managed to be poor yet be able to eat that much. I get her information and call the ministry lead. Before I know it, I hear the ministry lead walk through the church doors. She meets with this gal for quite a while. Maybe thirty or forty-five minutes. After the gal left crying, this ministry lead came in to fill me in on the results.

She proceeded to tell me she gave her a few gas cards. I asked why the gal left crying. She told me she asked the woman if she was a believer in Christ. The gal said yes. The ministry lead then began to share with her the importance of attending a home church so the brothers and sisters in Christ can help support her and pray for her. I guess this conversation convicted this lady to the point of tears. What I gathered from the situation was the ministry lead really felt like she was in need—in need of more than money. She needed Jesus.

When the ministry lead asked if she could pray for her, the gal asked if she could hold on to the ministry lead's hand for comfort. After holding her hand and praying for her, the gal said she really appreciated everything and her loving nature reminded her of her grandma.

It's all about the heart's attitude

For the longest time I thought charity was about generosity. I thought charity was about my actions. I thought charity was about having less so others can have more. What I've learned over the years is charity is not about my actions—it's a heart attitude.

When I looked at this lady, I saw a liar. I saw someone looking for a handout. Someone who knows churches have to be nice to people. In fact, I even thought she would pawn off the gift cards for drugs. What the Care Ministry lead saw was a beautiful soul in need of Jesus. It didn't matter how many teeth she had, how many cigarettes she smoked a day, or even if she was lying. She saw a genuine heart that really wanted someone to care for her, not judge her.

How dare me. How dare I be so focused on the surface. How dare I be a misrepresentation of Jesus in such a disgusting fashion. Let's just say, I spent a good amount of time after that seeking repentance. Charity is about the heart—like almost everything in our faith. The actions that come are merely biproducts of the heart's attitude.

I think about my problems giving money away in big cities. It's not about how much money I can give them. It's about my heart when I do it, and it's clear I didn't have the right heart. I think about picking up that check at Starbucks. I didn't have the right heart. I was trying to fulfill my own emotions. I think about the people I encounter in the church office. I didn't have a heart of charity. I had a heart full of junk. And the reason I don't want to take these needy people to buy them a meal is because I really don't care. I don't have the heart to. I merely have an obligation to my own conscience.

When I look back at my foolish heart's attitude toward charity, I realize if my heart had simply been in a better place, all of those situations would have been God glorifying. They could have been beautiful representations of God's love. Yet I turned God's temple into a marketplace for my own selfish desires.

RECONCILIATION WITH MYSELF

Only crazy people go to therapy. I know this to be true because most people who go to therapy talk loud and usually have weird twitches and strange collections of old dryer sheets. I also know this because I've gone to therapy very recently and went a fair amount of times growing up. I also talk loud, I'm pretty obsessive compulsive, and I cry a lot. To be fair, most of my crying comes from watching episodes of *Parenthood*.

Being crazy has its advantages because when you're crazy, no one takes you seriously; they just think you're weird. This means I can typically, in most situations, say what I want and it doesn't shock anyone. They just expect it because I'm crazy. I can also blame everything else I do on my craziness. When I do something that does take people off guard, most people tilt their heads back slightly in that moment of revelation and say, "Oh yeah, that's right. It's just Tony being Tony."

Most people who first meet me don't like me. I talk loud—and a lot—and it rubs people the wrong way. I'm used to it, so I tend to make the best of those situations. I usually say or do something ridiculous to help them arrive at the conclusion I'm crazy just a little bit quicker. This seems to be true of my entire family. As far back as I can remember, I've always known this to be true. At the dinner table, we never told stories, we acted them out loudly with very specific motions. We contemplated charging people to come watch the "Ziolko Dinner Theater." We were always the loud ones at family functions and with family friends we definitely talked the most. I know it's genetic because I watched the same thing happen to my mom. In social settings or meetings, anytime she spoke, everyone would look at her in the same way you look at the toddler who randomly talks to the adults in the middle of a conversation. Everyone just nods their heads and in a polite gesture, affirming what the child says, "Wow! That is really neat!" just to shut them up.

My mom is the most creative, beautiful person I know. In a different way than my wife of course. My mom is my inspiration and has always been my biggest fan. Not in a way most mothers are when their child is bad at Little League but they cheer them on anyway. She genuinely believed if I would just stop pouting, I could be a game changer, even if it wasn't from a clutch base hit or a home run. I could change the game with my attitude. And she was right.

My mom was always right and strong, so it always shocked me when family, friends, and people in meetings would treat her like she was a nuisance just because she talked a lot and was passionate. It not only shocked me, it broke my heart. And then I started to feel it on myself with my peers. People not taking me seriously.

I'll never forget a creative meeting I was in one time. We all sat there for a long time with no ideas. My mom always thrived in these situations. Even if her idea wasn't the best, it at least got everyone talking. So I offered up the best idea I could possibly offer in that moment. It wasn't great, and most likely not a keeper, but I figured it would at least get everyone talking. Everyone looked at me like that toddler I told you about, and their affirmations to my idea was much like that comment you give a little boy when he shows you his drawing from school, even though it's terrible. I got that similar, "Good job, little buddy!" from everyone as they simply went on disregarding any idea I had.

Window tint for transparency

I think what's difficult about not being liked by a lot of people is I'm a transparent person. I don't have multiple masks I wear to mold into certain situations like most people. I don't have a mask for work, friends, church, and home. Being a pastor, this has been a blessing and a curse. I'm the same person all the time. I act and say the same things from the stage at church that I would say in a bar drinking a beer with friends, and I certainly don't act differently at home. My wife can vouch for that.

That's the hardest part of this pill to swallow. When someone doesn't like me, it feels like they are basically saying to me they don't like the way I am as a father, spouse, pastor, and friend. Because I'm so transparent, it exposes me to the world for the most criticism—and they surely love to pile it on. It's not like I can just throw out that particular mask they don't like. Trust me, I've tried.

I wish I could change my transparency, I really do. I wish I wasn't so honest. I wish I was more politically-correct with my words and interactions, and I certainly wish more people liked me. And I wish people took me more seriously.

A knack for therapy

Most people develop the crazies. I've actually had it from a young age. In fact, I remember going to therapy even as a young boy. I grew up in what would be considered a normal Christian home. Dad worked, mom cooked dinner. As the only son, I played sports, my eldest sister was a cheerleader and in normal-youngest-sibling fashion, my little sister spent her days annoying me. We went to church every Sunday, pretended to like singing hymns, prayed before dinner, and talked a lot about God.

I remember the Christmas of my sixth-grade year when I finally got my first video game system. I had been waiting a few years to get that game system, and I was excited to play the football game with my dad. Christmas Day and the few days after that, Dad and I would lie on my bed with our feet at the pillows, facing the television playing video games nearly all day. Life couldn't have gotten any better. Then a few days after Christmas, I asked my dad if we could play some more video games. He told me yes, but said he needed to talk to Mom first. I ran up to my room and got the game set up while I waited.

After what felt like an hour, my parents came into my room and proceeded to inform me my dad was leaving. Now I didn't fully understand what they were saying. Where was he going? When would he be back? And when could we continue our video game? They explained to me Dad needed to move out of the house for a while, because he was not happy at home. I told him I was sorry for beating him in the video game and he didn't have to leave because of it. I promised him I would let him win next time.

It was a really difficult time for me as a twelve-year-old. Dad and I were close and had a lot of fun together. And after he left, things just became a lot different. Mom was crying all the time, and people were always at the house bringing us dinner like somebody had just died. But if I'm honest, as a twelve year old, I really didn't mind all the free pizza. As the months progressed, the cessation of my father living at home was becoming a reality. I started to learn the truth of the situation. I learned about the infidelity in their marriage, and I learned about his alcohol problems. My dad filed for divorce, my mom told him no.

Of course this affected me as a young boy. So to the best of my abilities, at the age of twelve, I began to act out. I became mean, rude, and destructive with my words. I would have acted mean in a physical way, but I was a wimp. It was then my mother decided to take me to a therapist. His name was Bruce, and he had a beard like Sigmund Freud. I didn't want to talk to him, so I sat in his office ignoring his questions. I decided I wouldn't say a word to the man. After a while, he asked me if I wanted a soda.

I said yes. Then he asked me about my video games. I told him I hated video games. When he asked why, I shrugged my shoulders and remembered I had decided to ignore him. After many visits with Bruce, I began to break down. He helped me figure out why I was mad and how to deal with it. I was astonished at the way he was able to figure me out. I decided, at the age of twelve, that I wanted to be a counselor, too.

The truth is . . .

I don't like myself. There it is, I said it. While that may have been difficult for me to say, I must confess this has been the hardest chapter I have ever written. In the process of writing this book, my mind and soul has gone through some tremendous healing and like usual, I cried a lot. Unfortunately, most of the crying took place in a public place like Starbucks. But this chapter . . . has wrecked me.

It's easy for me to sit down and talk about myself. We all like to talk about ourselves. But to sit down and attempt to elegantly piece together sentences that expose the hot mess I really am, telling everyone my insecurities, why I'm crazy, and the lies in my mind that weigh me down everyday to the point of defeat, has caused me significant weariness.

But the truth in all of this is I don't feel I'm a valuable person. I don't like my body type, the way I look, the fact I chew my nails, my personality, the way my voice sounds, the fact I have asthma and serious sinus issues. I don't like my OCD, I don't think I'm talented in any way, and I believe I'm average—at best.

My whole life I've always been average. My grades were always mediocre, my athletic ability was always average, my musical ability is average, I'm not fat, but I'm not skinny, so even my body type is average. My job salary is average, my biblical knowledge is annoyingly average. My memory is average. And I was never much of a ladies man. Even this book, has been difficult. My struggle throughout this entire process was what I had to say was average. And that since I'm an "average nobody," no one was going to read this. So what's the point of even completing this book when I know it's nothing special?

Heck, my own father abandoned me because he didn't want to be around me. Don't try to tell me, "He left your mom, not you," because we all know that's a load of crap. My mother made me, which means I'm half of her. So, if that's the reason he left, then I'm half of the person he hates anyway. I'm an average person who's easy to abandon.

I think all of this is what makes it so hard for me to be a husband, father, and pastor sometimes. It's hard for me to truly love my wife the way she needs to be loved or invest in my kids' lives when I don't see my own value. How can I truly see the blessing my wife is to me when I question why she would even want to be with me in the first place, let alone have children with me. My wife is hot, smart, and talented. She could be with a more attractive man, a man who makes more money, who doesn't have a small percentage of her musical ability. My wife could have married someone who doesn't have to have her father fix everything in our house because I don't know how to do any of it.

As a pastor, it's just as hard. How am I supposed to lead a congregation when I can't remember Scripture the way I'm supposed to? How am I supposed to lead a congregation closer to God when I have nothing to offer and no one takes me seriously? I've had leaders in churches tell me I wasn't worthy, skilled, or even in the right vocation. How am I supposed to show people how much God loves them, when sometimes I don't believe it myself?

I've been in a season of life that feels like I've been in all of my life. The season is I feel like I'm Timothy from the Bible and everyone else sees me as such. I want to reach the point where I'm Paul, pouring into Timothy, but it doesn't feel like I'll ever get there.

This recent trip to therapy was because of a transition in my life. I had just moved eleven-hundred miles away from both sets of parents, started a new job, bought a house, and became a father for the first time. All within a three month span. Needless to say my life was feeling chaotic.

When I started going to therapy, it started out with frustrations and difficulties of being a new father, a husband, and having a ministry. I thought I was having a hard time balancing the transitions.

I quickly realized why I was really there: because I didn't like myself and didn't feel like I was going to be able to break the cycle. I hated myself so much and didn't feel like I was any good at anything. I feared that I was going to fail in my duties and even worse, I didn't feel like I deserved to be a father, husband, or be a pastor. So much so I wanted to run away. I wanted to run to a comfort where my un-valuable, untalented self wouldn't be able to screw things up. Just like my dad did. And I hated myself even more for that. I was no better than him. I wanted to be a better person and there I was, dreaming of running away from it all, just like him.

Better together

My wife and I used to have just one car. When we first moved to Kansas, we decided to make the move with just one car. It started out as a temporary, purely financial decision that turned into something better. After several months, it became quite clear to us while very inconvenient with a new baby, my ever-changing work schedule, and her work schedule, we should stick with one car for as long as we could.

To our surprise, my wife and I noticed something in our marriage. We have the best conversations and discussions while driving. While living in Phoenix, a lot of nights, we would just hop in the car and drive into the desert country with no direction and just talk. Of course when we moved to Kansas with only one car, most days we were taking each other to work and picking each other up. It was amazing for our relationship. That extra twenty minutes each day in the car together was special to me, and I certainly didn't want to give it up.

Through the process of therapy and battling these feelings I was having, something came to mind and it help me pinpoint something that assisted in the beginning of my reconciliation with myself. It is dependency. It's not that Ashley is better than me or I'm so inferior. I realized that we are simply better to-gether.

The Ugly Couch

Reconciliation

The word "reconcile" means to go from hostility to friend-ship. This was my process. I knew if I was going to heal from all the things in my life; if I wanted to get rid of the ugliest couch I owned—the lies I believed from the enemy—I would have to begin the process of reconciliation with myself. I had to learn to stop hating myself, learn to have a friendship with myself, and to truly love myself for who I was. And at the same time, not settle for junk. God calls us to prune our branches and get rid of the ugly couches in our lives, but He doesn't identify us with them.

As I stated in the first chapter of this book, your identity doesn't have to be wrapped up in your wounds. You are not the person the enemy claims you are. Your worth isn't wrapped up in who you are not, but how God loves and calls you.

As we set to conclude this book, here's my final plea. We have gone through the filter in our own lives. We have taken the trash to the curb. This is great news, but what if there is one more step? Before you decide to close this book you must begin the process of reconciliation with yourself. Stop the hostility with yourself. Stop hating yourself and learn to befriend yourself.

God's love is so reckless and massive that even I am loved. Even you are loved. This is the greatest challenge for us in reconciliation: to simply believe in the gospel. That gospel is the same gospel where God speaks directly to us and shows us how much He loves us: the people He created Himself.

Are we comfortable living in hostility with the person God Himself created? Our greatest challenge is believing the gospel that outlines God's soaring love. It's the grace and love of God that is going to set us free . . . from ourselves. From the lies we choose to believe.

This entire book is wrapped around one concept; getting rid of the junk in your life you don't need. It's one thing to improve yourself emotionally and spiritually and another thing to try to be someone you are not.

Everything I've shared with you in this book isn't geared to change you into someone you are not. It's designed to help you see the person you already are in Jesus Christ and learn how to get rid of the junk hiding the beauty.

This is a process I have to go through every single day. Some days are better than others and some days I think, *I need more therapy.* I still believe while I may not be the most talented, I can still be a game changer with my attitude. But it's a process that keeps me focused on why I'm here on this earth in the first place: to love like Jesus did. And I can't love like Jesus if I don't love myself.

It's through reconciliation with ourselves we can truly start to see who God has made us to be. See, through reconciliation comes redemption and through redemption comes purpose. It's time to get rid of the junk in our lives hiding the beauty God made in us. And it's then, in that freedom we can fulfill our purpose.